Building on her previous work, *Beneath the Mask: Understanding Adopted Teens*, Debbie Riley and her C.A.S.E. Team have contributed another exciting and valuable book to the adoption clinical literature. The voices of adopted adolescents and young adults highlight various "stuck points" that are often emotional challenges as young people seek to integrate the adoption experience into their emerging sense of self. Each chapter provides exercises for the teen readers that clinicians can use with clients to help them process their thoughts and feelings about being adopted. C.A.S.E. has been in the forefront of adoption education, treatment, and clinical training. Their new book will undoubtedly be well received by the professional community and will foster more insightful and productive clinical work with adopted persons.

David Brodzinsky, PhD | Professor Emeritus
Developmental and Clinical Psychology
Rutgers University

As a father by adoption and an adoption professional for over 33 years, I've learned that when people who were adopted speak, it's time to listen closely to what they have to share— and learn from their real-life experiences. *Beneath the Mask: For Teen Adoptees* provides a diverse group of adoptees the opportunity to share their individual adoption story in their own words and from their own perspective in order to educate, encourage, and give others who were adopted (and their families) a better understanding of what it means and feels like to be adopted.

Chuck Johnson | President and CEO
National Council For Adoption

Beneath the MASK:

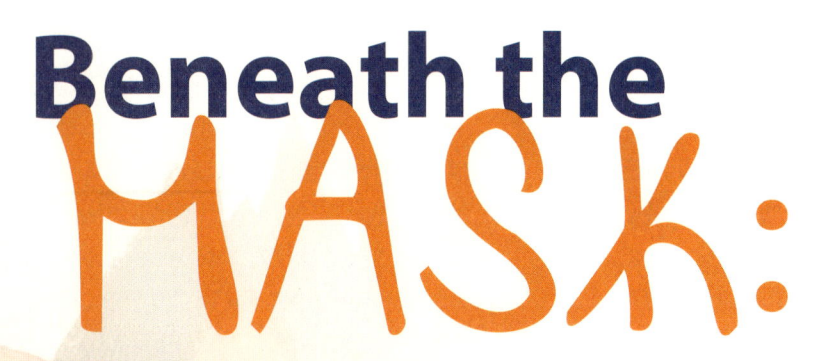

For Teen Adoptees

Teens and Young Adults
Share Their Stories

C.A.S.E.
the nonprofit
CENTER FOR ADOPTION
SUPPORT AND EDUCATION
since 1998

nurture.
inspire.
empower.

Center for Adoption
Support and Education

Beneath the Mask: For Teen Adoptees
Teens and Young Adults Share Their Stories

Published by Center for Adoption Support and Education (C.A.S.E.)
Copyright © 2019 by Center for Adoption Support and Education (C.A.S.E.)
All Rights Reserved. No part of this book may be reproduced or transmitted in any form or by any means, graphic electronic, or mechanical, including photocopying, recording, taping, or by any information storage or retrieval system—except by a reviewer who may quote brief passages in a review to be printed in a magazine, newspaper, or on the web—without written permission from C.A.S.E.

Cover and interior design: Susan Oslund, BlueSkyDesignWorks.com
Illustrator: Paige Billin-Frye
Copy editor: Olivia Miller
Mask photographer: Meryl Trachtman
Cover mask art: created by Jake
Title page mask art: created by Carrie

ISBN-13: 978-0-578-46529-6

We dedicate this book
to the thousands of children, teens and adults who are adopted and their families whom we have been honored to support since opening our doors in 1998. You have taught us so much as we continue to nurture, inspire and empower those we serve.

—The C.A.S.E. Team

Being a teenager is full of adventure, growing independence, fears and more. Add adoption to this mix and you sometimes have even more questions and unknowns. The power of being able to say, "I know exactly how you feel," is incredible. *Beneath the Mask: For Teen Adoptees* is just that—for teens who are adopted. To hear about the winding path of others can be a beacon on your own path. I wish I had this resource when I was growing up!

Rebecca Jones Gaston | adoptee

As an adult adoptee working in child welfare—and someone who is still very much traveling my own adoption journey—I loved this book. *Beneath the Mask: For Teen Adoptees* offers real and genuine utility through the art of storytelling. The articulate narratives offered by these teen and young adult writers constitutes a remarkable gift to a population that so badly wants to be understood and feel a connection. Written with authority and wisdom, each of these contributing writers generously captures the complex texture of the very real and incredibly personal emotional challenges adoptees encounter on their journey. With a truly thoughtful treatment of some of the most common themes related to the lived adoption experience, Debbie Riley and the C.A.S.E. Team have produced a valuable resource, complete with hands-on tools and space for journaling in a unique and penetrating format. Maximum praise for this powerful book, for these insightful writers, and for the Center for Adoption Support and Education for giving the adolescent adoption community a wonderfully experiential platform.

Matthew R. McGuire | adoptee

For any adoptee who is missing information about their life, struggles with their identity, wonders why they needed to be adopted or simply wonders if they belong, this book connects you with 20 other adoptees in their teens and early adulthood who understand these stuck points. It wasn't until adulthood that I was able to feel the power of connecting with other adoptees, and it changed my life. Being with others of a shared experience is powerful. Bravo!

Angela Tucker | adoptee
www.theadoptedlife.com

Acknowledgements

The C.A.S.E. Team is deeply grateful to the talented adoptees who shared their heartfelt personal stories to help other adoptees to feel that they are not alone. These contributors also created their masks whose photographs are portrayed with their stories: Amnoni, Anna, Annabeth, Carrie, Cheyenne, Daniel, David, Emily, Jake, Leah, Naomi, Ottilie, Rachel, Ren, Sara, Skyler, Tatyana, Teresa, Zahra, and Zoe.

The C.A.S.E. Team

Debbie Riley | LCMFT, CEO

Ellen Singer | LCSW-C, Sr. Therapist & Training Coordinator, Chief Editor

Melisa Rogers | BA, Director of Marketing

Barb Franck | LCSW-C, Adoption-Competent Therapist

Mari Itzkowitz | LCSW, Director of Clinical Services

Susan LaVigna | LCSW-C, Adoption-Competent Therapist

Penny Zimmerman | LCSW-C, Clinical Supervisor

Teens and young adults have contributed their personal stories in this book and some content may contain sensitive material.

Table of Contents

Introduction: Letter to Teens by Debbie Riley, C.A.S.E. CEO 7
   What Are the "Six Stuck Spots?" 9

Stuck Spot #1: *Identity* 10
   Stories 11
   Activity: Make Your Mask 20
   Journal: The Meaning of Your Mask 21
   Exercise: Out of My Head and Into the Box 23

Stuck Spot #2: *Difference* 24
   Stories 25
   Activity: Find a Song 36
   Journal: Reflections on Your Song 37
   Exercise: Use Your 5 Senses 39

Stuck Spot #3: *Missing or Difficult Information* 40
   Stories 41
   Activity: Puzzle Pieces 50
   Journal: What I Want to Know 52
   Exercise: Relaxation Playlist 54

Stuck Spot #4: *Reason for Adoption* 55
   Stories 56
   Activity: Finding the Words Puzzle 65
   Journal: Letter to Your Birth Parents 66
   Exercise: Safe Space 68

Stuck Spot #5: *Loyalty* 69
   Stories 70
   Activity: Personal Constellation 76
   Journal: Reflections on Connections 78
   Exercise: Balloon 80

Stuck Spot #6: *Permanence* 81
   Stories 82
   Activity: Graffiti on Boulder 88
   Journal: What Feels Permanent 90
   Exercise: Letter From Your Future Self 92

Final Thoughts 93

Notes, Scribbles, Doodles, etc. 94

About C.A.S.E. 95

Introduction

A Letter to Teens by Debbie Riley | C.A.S.E. CEO

Dear Teens,

I am certain you would agree that adolescence is a time of new experiences and challenges with many ups and downs. It is often filled with normal worries, fears, and insecurities. Being adopted can pose unique challenges during this incredible time in your life. This book was written to help you make sense of these challenges, see that you are not alone, and know that you can get through them.

When I knew I wanted to be a therapist, I also knew that I wanted to work with teenagers. I enjoy your creativity, spirit, honesty, no-nonsense attitude, and the work involved to earn your trust. I love being part of your journey toward understanding more about who you are, your self-acceptance, and how you solve problems.

In 1991, my husband and I adopted our wonderful son. Becoming an adoptive parent sparked my curiosity about the world of teens who are adopted. I dedicated myself to learning everything I could. I started listening to teens I was working with very carefully. I learned that everyone in your life needs to understand your conflicted thoughts and feelings about being adopted.

In 1993, I met another adoptive mom, Kathleen Dugan. From the time she was in middle school, Kathleen knew that she wanted to adopt someday. After giving birth to four daughters, Kathleen and her husband Mike adopted eight older children from foster care. Together, Kathleen and I founded the Center for Adoption Support and Education (C.A.S.E.)—a place where adoption is understood and anyone connected to adoption can get the support they need. We believe that, "Talking is good for everyone," and that open communication is key and secrets are harmful.

Since 1998, I have worked with hundreds of teens who joined their families through adoption. They have shared their innermost thoughts about what adoption means to them and what they find challenging about being adopted. They have told me how much they love their adoptive families; how sad they sometimes feel when they think about their birth families including their desire to connect with them someday.

Of major importance, the teens taught me how desperately they wanted to be understood by parents, siblings, teachers, coaches, and friends. So, in 2005, I wrote *Beneath the Mask: Understanding Adopted Teens*, co-authored with a wonderful colleague who also loved teens, Dr. John Meeks. In our book, we share that teens' emotional challenges center on **six themes** related to the adoption experience. I call them the "**six stuck spots**." They are:

1) **Identity**
2) **Difference**
3) **Missing or Difficult Information**
4) **Reason for Adoption**
5) **Loyalty**
6) **Permanence**

The teens working through these stuck spots often felt alone and misunderstood. I knew they had so much to offer other teens who may be struggling. So, we invited teens and young adults connected to C.A.S.E. to be part of creating a new publication that would be a "companion" book to my original book. Our request was met with great enthusiasm and gratitude for the opportunity to be helpful to you. So, here it is: *Beneath the Mask: For Teen Adoptees...Teens and Young Adults Share Their Stories.*

We asked the writers to choose a "stuck spot" they felt personally challenged by and describe their experiences including what helped them "get to the other side." The writers are both male and female, and represent a diversity of adoption experiences; some were adopted through foster care, others through private adoption agencies in the U.S., and still others through international sources. They come from single-parent families, two-parent families, divorced families, LGBTQ families, kinship, and transracial adoptive families.

What you will find in the book:

Included in each chapter is an explanation and discussion of one of the six stuck spots, followed by the stories of our contributing writers, highlighting their struggles with that spot. It is important to note that while a writer may focus on one spot, challenges around other stuck spots may be described as well.

The stories are followed by suggested activities and exercises, including space to journal, and are intended to help you:

1) creatively express your thoughts and feelings

2) reflect upon your personal experience with each stuck spot

3) learn new ways of coping with powerful emotions

I hope you will find this book helpful and know that you are not alone in your thoughts and feelings as an adoptee.

I wish you all the best on your journey. Thank you for taking us along with you.

Sincerely,

Debbie

Debbie Riley | LCMFT, CEO
Center for Adoption Support and Education

The Six Stuck Spots

As they are growing up, many adoptees struggle with issues connected to their adoption experience. Hundreds of teens have come to the Center for Adoption Support and Education (C.A.S.E.) for help. Through working with them, we learned that their lives were seriously impacted by consistent patterns where they felt emotionally "stuck." Their struggles included feelings of low self-worth, deep desires to seek information about why they were adopted, and confusion as to whether they did something to cause being placed for adoption. Some teens struggled with trying to figure out who they were when they had little or no information about their past and who brought them into the world.

We invite you to read a description of each of the six stuck spots with highlights of the typical questions, thoughts and feelings that reflect struggles with that spot. Think about whether you identify with any of the statements or questions. As you read about each "spot" and the stories that follow, think about if and where **you** might be stuck.

Before you begin

We know that as you read these stories and work through this book, some strong feelings may come up for you. You might feel sad, angry, confused, or frightened. Painful and troubling memories may be triggered. We suggest that you identify at least one trusted friend and one trusted adult (a parent, school counselor, or therapist) who you can talk to and share your experience with along the way. Think of someone who you believe can provide you with support and comfort.

Here are names and phone numbers of friends/adults I trust and can talk to about important stuff:

_____
NAME OF TRUSTED ADULT   TEL #

_____
NAME OF FRIEND   TEL #

_____
NAME OPTIONAL   TEL #

Identity

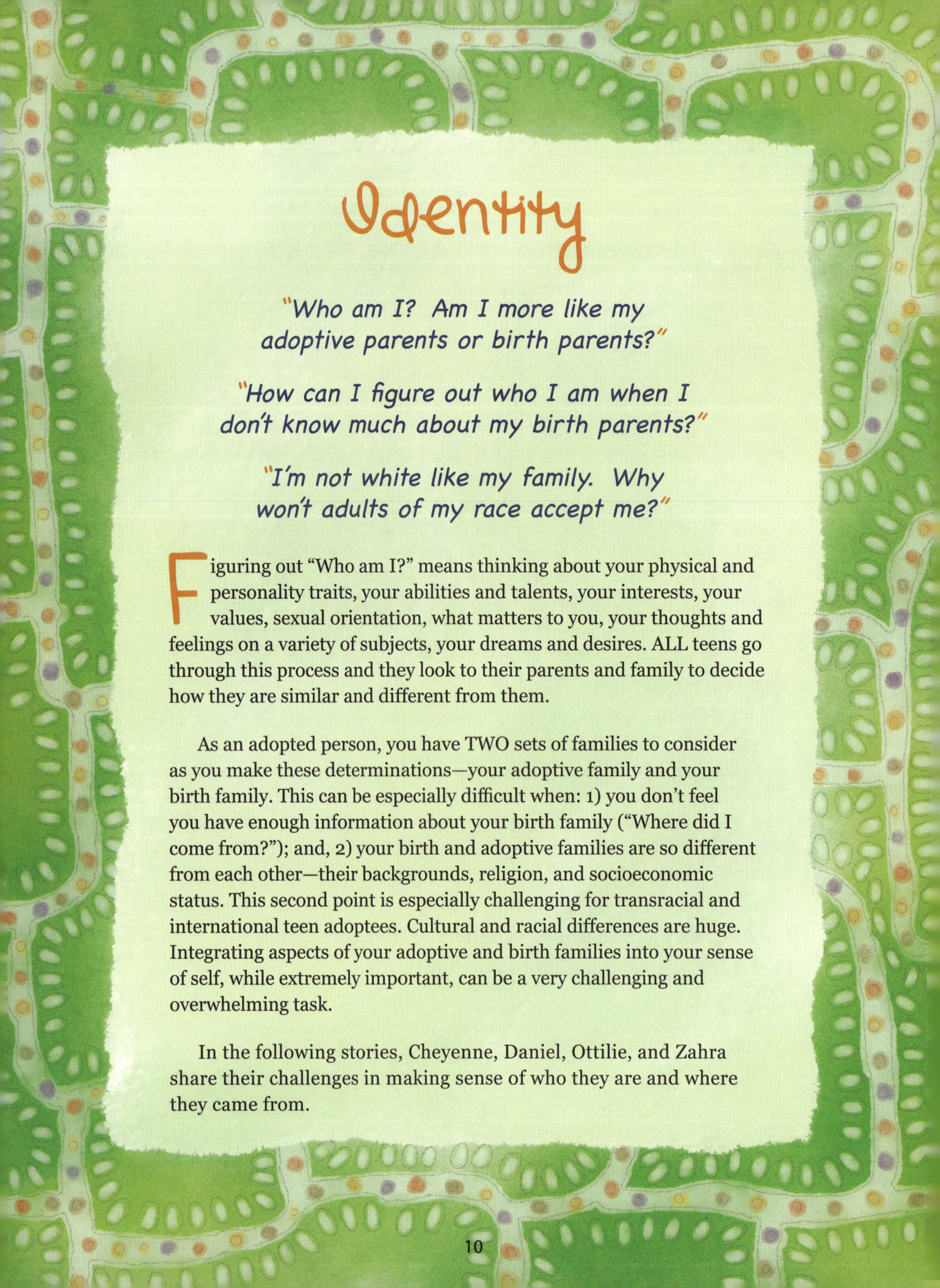

"Who am I? Am I more like my adoptive parents or birth parents?"

"How can I figure out who I am when I don't know much about my birth parents?"

"I'm not white like my family. Why won't adults of my race accept me?"

Figuring out "Who am I?" means thinking about your physical and personality traits, your abilities and talents, your interests, your values, sexual orientation, what matters to you, your thoughts and feelings on a variety of subjects, your dreams and desires. ALL teens go through this process and they look to their parents and family to decide how they are similar and different from them.

As an adopted person, you have TWO sets of families to consider as you make these determinations—your adoptive family and your birth family. This can be especially difficult when: 1) you don't feel you have enough information about your birth family ("Where did I come from?"); and, 2) your birth and adoptive families are so different from each other—their backgrounds, religion, and socioeconomic status. This second point is especially challenging for transracial and international teen adoptees. Cultural and racial differences are huge. Integrating aspects of your adoptive and birth families into your sense of self, while extremely important, can be a very challenging and overwhelming task.

In the following stories, Cheyenne, Daniel, Ottilie, and Zahra share their challenges in making sense of who they are and where they came from.

Cheyenne, 18

It was the longest car ride ever. The night was cold, the autumn leaves had fallen from the trees and the snow on the ground disappeared that year. I soon drifted off into a deep soothing sleep. When I woke up, there were tall skinny townhouses with different types of families living in them. As we stepped out of the car, we approached a house with a dark green metal door that was soon to be my new home.

I was born in Minnehaha, South Dakota. My birth and adoptive families are Caucasian. Andrew, my twin, and I were the youngest of four children. At some point during my early childhood, my biological family moved to the D.C. area to be closer to family. My parents had problems with drugs, and my family was often homeless. We sometimes lived in houses where my biological dad worked in construction. At one time, I recall living in his construction van with my siblings for months on end. Later, when I was about six years old, my biological parents went to jail because of drug use, so my aunt took us in.

Andrew and I went with my Auntie Di, and my brother, Sean, and sister, Shelbi, went with Aunt Donna. I lived with my Auntie Di on and off for a few years. Then suddenly, one day, my brother and I came home from school and saw that my aunt had packed all our stuff into boxes. She told us that a lady was coming to take us to our new family. (I didn't understand at that young age that living with my aunt was just a temporary situation until we could be placed in a foster-to-adopt home.) We waited patiently for this mysterious lady to come and before I knew it, I saw a funny looking woman with dark black hair standing in the doorway. We put our boxes in her car and said goodbye to our Auntie Di, leaving to go meet our new family. I was so sad and my heart sank when later, we were told that we might never see our aunt again.

We rang the doorbell to the small townhouse. A beautiful woman with blonde hair and a tall man with just a little bit of hair opened the green door. The first thing I remember asking them was, *"Are you gonna be my new mommy and daddy?"* They both smiled and gave us a big, welcoming hug. I had a feeling that our new family was going to be our last. We went on to have such great memories in this new house. My favorite memory was building forts out of blankets in the basement and grabbing our sleeping bags, flashlights, teddy bears and books so that we could spend the whole night acting like cavemen.

It took years to finalize our adoption. There were a variety of visits we had to go to, many court dates, and so much fighting over two little 9-year-old kids who just wanted to be loved and taken care of. It was a confusing time, and I remember asking myself, "Why me?"

I chose to write about IDENTITY because it is the stuck spot that has impacted me the most. Most adopted kids who I know don't know anything about their birth family history, but I think sometimes I know too much! And the things I know sometimes make knowing who I am very complicated. I worry about the fact that my birth parents both have bipolar disorder and addiction problems. I don't know if these problems could be passed on to me and I don't want to end up like they did. Fortunately, I also know several positive characteristics about my birth parents and extended birth family relatives; they are intelligent, musically talented, and have a great sense of humor.

When I look at my own positive traits, I know I am honest, hardworking, have a great sense of humor, and am musically talented, too! Although I went through many struggles with my biological family, I'm still who I am today because of them. Music plays a big role in my biological dad's life; he loves playing the guitar and listening to music. I inherited my musical talent from him; I now sing in both my school and church choirs.

My adoptive parents helped me develop into the strong, independent woman I am. They taught me to be honest and to do what's right. I have always practiced my birth family's religious faith, and this eventually influenced my adoptive family to also attend church. I think I developed a sense of humor because of my birth family, but my adoptive family keeps it going as they are funny, too. My adoptive parents taught me to always work hard and strive to be the best in life and to never let anything bring me down. My older biological sister and brother never had the chance to attend college, so one of my goals is to be the first child in my birth family to graduate from college. I plan to become a teacher because I want to make an impact on children's lives, especially those who may have experienced the same challenges that I have faced.

As I have struggled to figure out my identity and what parts of my birth family, my adoptive family and myself contributed to who I am, I faced other challenges as well. My mom and my therapist helped me get over my depression. They were by my side the whole time, never giving up on me.

Today I can say that I know who I am and who I want to be. I know what my goals are and what I want to achieve in the future. From this process, I've learned that music, God, and my family play a huge role in my life.

Finally, family is a huge part of my life. In my adoptive family, I have three younger brothers that mean the world to me, two adopted from foster care and a foster brother. I want to be a good role model for them. My mom and dad are the best parents anyone could ask for. My mom is cool, up-to-date and just wonderful, which brings us closer. My dad may get on my nerves, but I love him; he goes out of his way to make me happy.

My advice to adoptive parents: Tell your kids their story, including where they came from and even details that might be difficult. If they have questions, answer them honestly. Give them information when you think they are ready to hear it, but do not keep anything from them.

I'd like to give this advice to other adopted kids: You shouldn't be afraid to tell your story. Don't be afraid to be yourself, and whether you have some of your traits from your biological parents or your adoptive parents, embrace who you are no matter where you came from. You may question if your life is worth it, and it is. No matter what you went through, your life will always be worth it. I believe that your biological parents love you whether or not you believe it. They wanted your life to be better with your adoptive parents because they knew your adoptive parents would give you a better life than they could. A life full of love, laughter, and happiness. Trust me, I used to ask myself all the time—why did this have to happen to me? Why did I have to go through all of this, and remember ALL of what happened? I really feel now that being adopted is the best thing that has ever happened to me and I wouldn't trade it for anything in the world. My name is Cheyenne and I love the fact that I'm adopted.

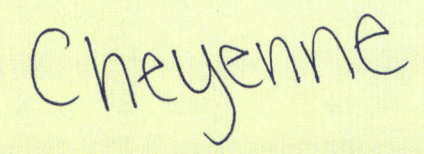

Cheyenne

Daniel, 20

I was born into a family who didn't have anything—to a birth mother who hadn't even finished high school, and a birth father who was an illegal immigrant from Puebla, Mexico, and who physically abused my birth mother. Because of this abuse, my birth mother took my older sister and me and ran away with another man. When I was about a year old, my birth mother and this man had a child together. Feeling overwhelmed, my birth mother gave me to friends who promised to take care of me and keep me safe. But the people who promised to take care of me—the people whom a toddler depended on for safety—abused me.

The turning point in my life was when social service workers removed me from that situation and placed my siblings and me in foster care. When the social workers found me, I had been beaten from head to toe and had cigarette burns on my body. (The burns were so bad that both the doctors and my adoptive parents were surprised that I had no lasting scars.) With my brother's need to receive specialized care, my sister and I were first taken to an emergency foster care home, then to another home, and eventually to a group home run by a nun where we experienced nothing but kindness. After about a year, we were placed in my parents' home as foster children, and then adopted by them. All of this happened before I was two and a half years old.

It starts with a language I barely learned and usually ends with my perfected phrase of "*No hablo Español.*" When strangers approach me, and assume I speak Spanish because they think I look Hispanic, it's not just a misunderstanding, but a reminder of a part of my identity that I have no connection to.

When I was placed in foster care, I was too young to remember anything about my birth parents. My birth mom is Caucasian and my birth father is from Mexico. Although I see my birth mother three times a year, I have not seen my birth father since I was an infant. So, when I ask myself whether I'm more like my birth parents or my adoptive parents, the question is always unanswerable. It depresses me to think about it because when I entered foster care, I didn't just lose part of my biological family (I was raised with my birth sister), but also a big part of my family history, and therefore, a big part of my identity.

I wonder, for instance, whether my personality or habits are like my birth father's or like anyone on his side of my birth family. I have asked my birth mother some questions and looked at some photos, but it has never been enough for me to satisfy my needs.

One way I have learned to cope with this feeling of loss is to have faith in my birth mother's decision to run away with her children from my abusive birth father, believing that he wouldn't be good for my life. It is through the understanding that she needed to keep us safe from him that I find some peace in never knowing him.

Another part of my identity that I have struggled to accept and cope with is being a victim of child abuse. Although I know that I wasn't hit for doing something wrong and I didn't deserve what was done to me, the fact is that my experience has left me with a haunting feeling of doubt and unexplainable pain. When I first thought about being abused, I couldn't accept it. I couldn't even call it abuse and I never wanted to talk about it. I would do everything I could think of to avoid the topic because of how disturbing it was to me. But I guess that's the point—something that painful isn't supposed to be easy to think about, let alone talk about. Now, after working to understand my feelings, I can acknowledge that despite the abuse, I am alive. I am a survivor and I can overcome this pain and any difficult situation that I encounter going forward.

Daniel

"A Message to the Haunted"
(Daniel's message to anyone who has been abused.)

We are the abused. Whether a child is abused physically or emotionally, whether or not a child will ever know their abuser, chances are it haunts them. It is not always physical scars. It can be hard to put into words, but it is a constant feeling of doubt or pain that can follow anyone after the fact. It is my personal belief that even when a child is adopted, this constant feeling is not likely to dissipate and may, in fact, cause more unintended pain beneath the surface if the child is unable to gain closure. It will inevitably leave someone with many questions: *Why was I hurt? Who hurt me and where are they now? Will I ever be hurt like that again? What am I supposed to do with my feelings right now?* Sometimes these questions can go unanswered and leave behind a feeling of doubt that we have no idea how to deal with and the people around us have no idea how to help us cope with. Sometimes all you need is another person who has also been hurt to tell you they understand how you feel, without asking you to describe a single word of it. If you are reading this and were abused, it means two things: you are not alone and you are not a victim, but a survivor. As a person, you have the ability to acknowledge the difference and take control of whatever feelings are left behind after you have survived the pain.

Ottilie, 15

I was adopted at two weeks old. My mother had been looking for a little girl to adopt for the longest time and was so happy to finally hold me in her arms. My birth mother loved having me inside her for nine months, and trusted that my adoptive mom would take great care of me. I've never met my dad, and don't know anything about him. I met my birth mom, of course, when I was a baby, but, of course, I don't remember anything. I was blessed to be put in a good home, and I'm thankful every day for what I have. However, there are always going to be hard parts about adoption, and for me, it is about "Difference" and "Identity."

Difference. That is something I deal with every day. I am a 5'3" medium brown skinned, beautiful African-American girl with kinky brown hair. My mom is a 5'7" white female with silky straight, short brown hair. So, yeah, there is one difference. The other is our age. I am almost 16, and my mom is 63. It is hard sometimes trying to make her understand the way I think, the fact that I need to get my hair done, the clothes and shoes I want, and the way things fit my body. It's a struggle. She has learned to understand me somewhat better, but sometimes I feel that she hasn't tried to understand me as well as she could. She is my opposite, and this causes great difficulty.

Identity has been a big challenge for me. I'm uniquely different from my mom, and everyone else I know. It's hard sometimes to fit in. I have my black group of friends, and my white group of friends, my Hispanic group of friends, and my mixed group of friends. Some black people say I act white. Well, I don't think you can act a color. I have too many groups of friends to be acting like a certain color. I'm friends with African-Americans, Africans, Asians, Caucasians, Hispanics, and people of mixed races.

Through everything I have been through, I have had people to help me cope. For example, my mother's friend has been my mentor since I was about nine years old. She's been there through everything...my tough times and good times. Another way I coped was through my friends. I don't know what I would do without my friends. They have been there since I can remember. Many of them know about my past, and have helped to liven my spirits many times. My C.A.S.E. therapist has helped my mother and me with our many conflicts. He gives us advice about what we should work on, and how we can change what we were previously doing. He listens to both sides of the story to see how he can be of help. Sometimes I have been very upset and have found it difficult to cope.

If you have similar struggles with your parents, just know it's not only you! I've dealt with this problem forever. The worst part about being different is when my mom and I are together in public. Having people stare at us is not uncommon, but I'm used to it by now and it doesn't bother me as much as it used to. The very worst part about being different comes up for me around my boyfriends. It's always hard for a boy to meet my mom. It's the scariest part of my relationship. I get scared that when he meets her he might think of me differently, that he will have difficulty accepting how different my family is. However, I try hard to remember that if he is willing to meet my mom and if he really cares for me, he will accept me and my mother for who we are. I also want to say that being different has some advantages. For example, when my mom and I are walking in the city, I can act totally independent, and nobody would ever know that we are together. I feel free and like I can do anything. So, believe me, difference isn't always a bad thing.

I know that I do not want my identity to reflect my adoptive mother's identity. It really bothers me when people compare me to her, as we are two different people and it will always be that way. There are so many things that make me ME. I have played the viola since fourth grade. I learned to swim at a very young age and I have been dancing for 11 years. My favorite sport is tennis and my second favorite sport is soccer, and I am a huge social bug. My style, my swag can never be bagged, my skills to make thrills will never get lagged. BARZ. Peace, I'm out, never forget to never be ashamed to be you!

Ottilie

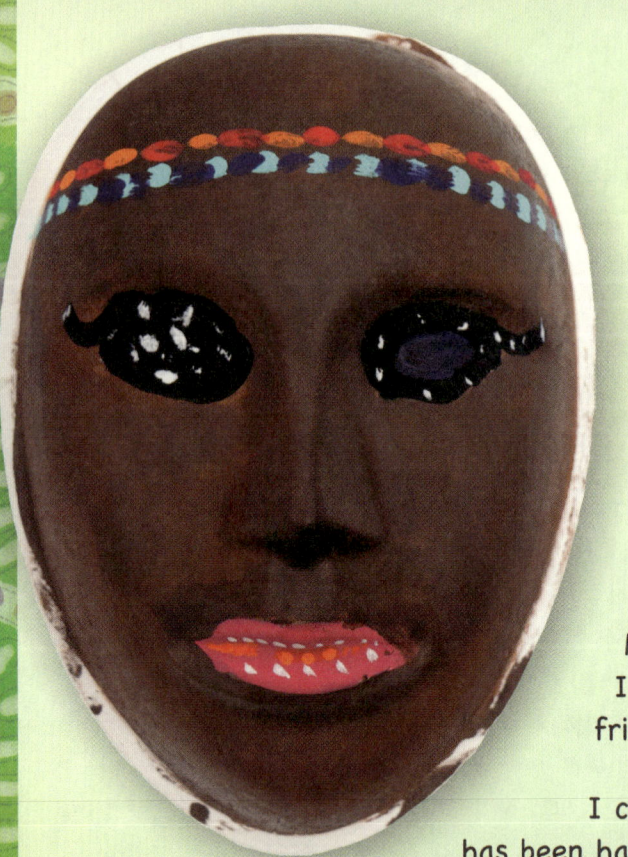

Zahra, 14

Who am I?

I'm Zahra and I am 14 years old and in the eighth grade. I was adopted when I was about six months old. I am from Mozambique in Africa. My parents are Caucasian. I love art, music (hip-hop, Bob Marley, and pop), the ocean, and doing hair. I also love spending time with my family and friends.

I chose Identity as my stuck spot because it has been hard for me to figure out who I am when there have been so many changes in my life that I couldn't control. I have always wondered a lot about my early life and my story. *Why did my birth family give me away, and was there a good reason? Did they not want me?* All I know is that my birth mom was sick and couldn't take care of me. Nobody knows anything about my birth dad or other family members.

I look very different from the rest of my family. I am curvy, have curly hair, dark skin, a round nose, and light eyebrows. Sometimes when I am at a restaurant or a store with my family, people will ask my parents if I am with them. Sometimes they ask us if my parents are going to pay for me. You get the point—people can't tell if I am part of my family group because I look so different from them. Strangers aren't the only ones who question me; I question myself, too.

Life became more complicated when I started middle school. I felt that people began to treat me differently, and I wasn't sure if it was because of my actions or my looks. I had a hard time because I wanted to be like my friends who knew who their birth family was because they lived with them! Not knowing my birth family made me feel confused and depressed. I felt very alone, like I was the only person with this problem and it was me against my friends, my family and the world.

I wondered a lot about what would have happened if I had not been adopted. I thought about what would happen if I found my birth family. *Would they look like me, be like me, act like me? Would they welcome me in? Would my adoptive family let me meet this family that I have missed, or would they be scared or worried, and not let me go?*

Sometimes I wonder if I look more like my birth mom or birth dad. I wonder if I will ever know. I have never met anyone who I am biologically related to, but I wish that I had. Sometimes I want to find them so I can know more about myself, my family history and birth culture...so I can see how I am like my birth family.

There are a few people who shined a light in my dark area. These people told me that I am NOT alone, that there are many people who are just like me who are asking the same questions. They helped me open up about my past and showed me that I am still the girl who loves to smile, laugh, and enjoy the ocean. They helped me see that I was just growing up a bit. My family, friends, therapist, and a special teacher helped me to learn that you can't always figure things out for yourself; sometimes you need an extra push or someone to point you in the right direction. They taught me that there are always going to be mysteries in life, and you're not always going to have all the answers, but you can still have a great life.

I would like other adopted kids to know that sometimes you might feel like you are the only kid who has unanswered questions, but you're not. I want parents and teachers to know that middle school is the time when kids notice differences between themselves and other kids that may not have been important in elementary school. Coping with this awareness can be very difficult and your kids need your love and support.

Zahra

ACTIVITY Make Your Mask

As an adoptee, you have many thoughts and feelings about who you are, where you came from, what you want to share with others about yourself, how you see yourself, and how you believe or want others to see you. We all, in effect, wear a "mask," choosing to show or not show different parts of ourselves. Think about what you want the world to see when looking at you and, using colored pencils or markers, draw it on the mask. Be as creative as you want. There is no wrong way, no right way. Be thoughtful about the colors you choose and what they represent to you.

ACTIVITY Make Your Mask

Journal   The Meaning of Your Mask

Think about what you chose to portray on your mask. Describe it. What do the colors represent to you? What does the design represent? Think about what you chose not to show on your mask. What did you choose to leave off and why? Where do you think these different parts of your mask came from? What parts feel like they are from your birth family, what parts from your adoptive family, and what feels like it's uniquely you?

Journal...continued

Exercise
Out of My Head and Into the Box

Find a small box and decorate it if you like.

This box is going to become a container for any thoughts or feelings that are bothering you, so keep it handy, along with some small pieces of paper and a pen or pencil.

Whenever something is worrying or upsetting you, write it down on one of the pieces of paper and put it in your box.

Now you won't have to think about it; it is safely in your box, and out of your head.

If you're at school or away from home when something pops into your head that needs to go in the box, you can still write it down and put it in the box when you get home.

> **BONUS:** When your box feels full, challenge yourself to throw the pieces of paper away without reading them. Really let them go.

Difference

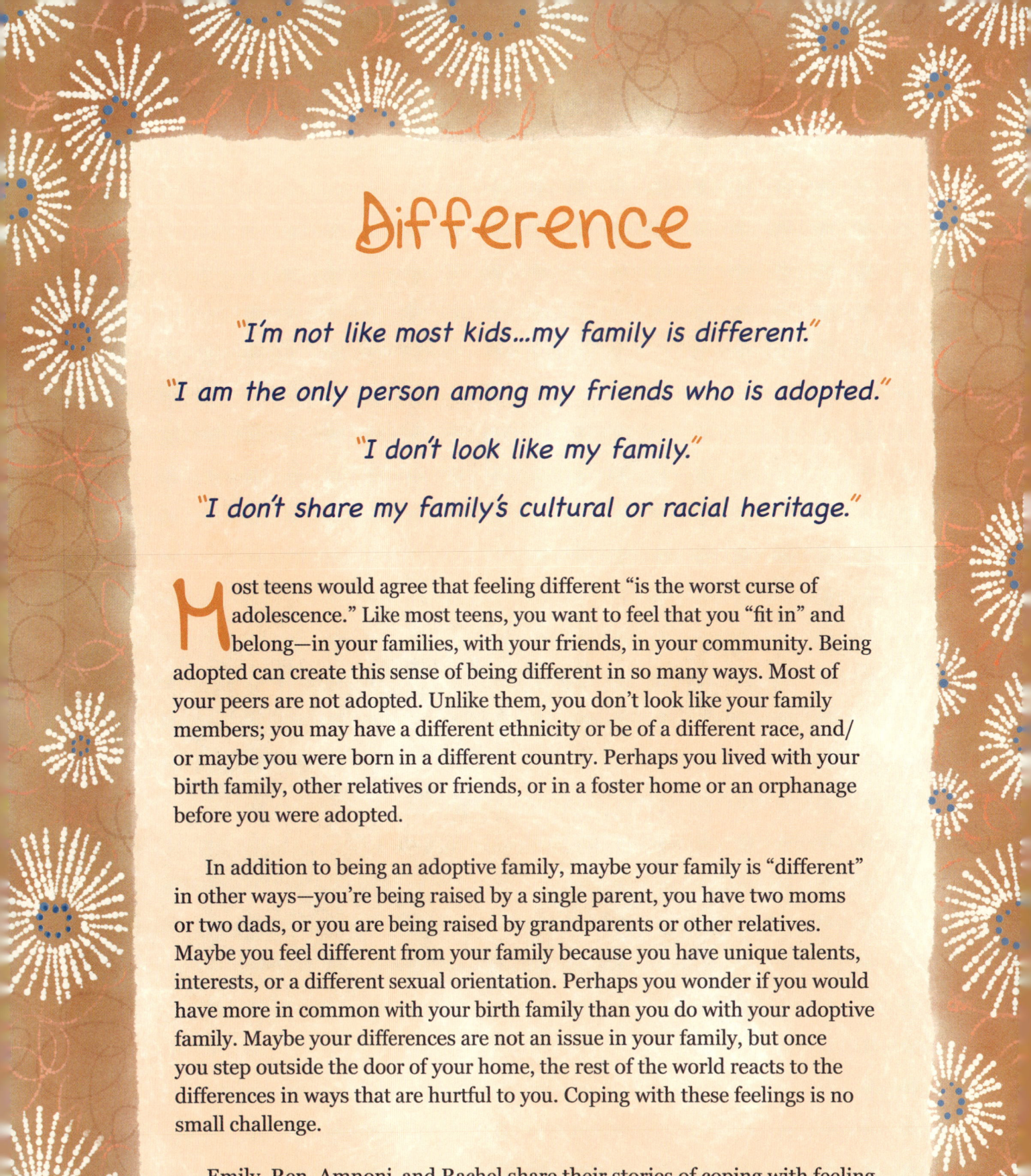

"I'm not like most kids...my family is different."

"I am the only person among my friends who is adopted."

"I don't look like my family."

"I don't share my family's cultural or racial heritage."

Most teens would agree that feeling different "is the worst curse of adolescence." Like most teens, you want to feel that you "fit in" and belong—in your families, with your friends, in your community. Being adopted can create this sense of being different in so many ways. Most of your peers are not adopted. Unlike them, you don't look like your family members; you may have a different ethnicity or be of a different race, and/or maybe you were born in a different country. Perhaps you lived with your birth family, other relatives or friends, or in a foster home or an orphanage before you were adopted.

In addition to being an adoptive family, maybe your family is "different" in other ways—you're being raised by a single parent, you have two moms or two dads, or you are being raised by grandparents or other relatives. Maybe you feel different from your family because you have unique talents, interests, or a different sexual orientation. Perhaps you wonder if you would have more in common with your birth family than you do with your adoptive family. Maybe your differences are not an issue in your family, but once you step outside the door of your home, the rest of the world reacts to the differences in ways that are hurtful to you. Coping with these feelings is no small challenge.

Emily, Ren, Amnoni, and Rachel share their stories of coping with feeling different, and their experiences with the outside world, including racism.

Emily, 21

When I was 15 months old I was adopted from an orphanage in China. Growing up, I always knew my family appeared different—I am Asian and both of my parents are Caucasian. To further add to the abnormality, it was just my mom and me for most of my life, since my parents divorced when I was young. It was no secret to me that I was adopted. There was no "big reveal" or attempts to hide it; I just always knew. Most of the time, being adopted didn't faze me, and I was never really ashamed or embarrassed by it from what I can remember.

I am fortunate to have grown up in an area that is so diverse. I think this made being adopted somewhat easier. The fact that there were so many people of different races and ethnicities in my classes at school made being Asian with white parents a little more "normal." Living in such a diverse area, just being Asian did not affect me as compared to more recent times when I find myself in a room where I am the only person who is a different race.

People's curiosity about adopted people involves questions about our birthplace, birth parents, and if we are ever going to try to find them. I don't know if I am different from the average adopted teen, but I personally have not yet felt any desire to reconnect with China, my birthplace or my birth parents. It's not something that I have ever really thought about. Even though I felt insecure about the makeup of my family when attending school events, the desire to know more about where I am from has never been an interest of mine. I think I feel this way because of how my adoptive family made me feel growing up.

Shortly after I was adopted, my parents divorced and my dad moved out. Although you can't know what you're missing if you never had it, I never felt like I was missing something or that I didn't belong in my adoptive family. Both sides of my family have always treated me as if I was my parents' biological daughter. My mom always made it clear to me that no matter what, she was my mom and she would say, "I may not be your birth mother, but I am still your mother." It wasn't that I didn't believe it, but sometimes I needed reassurance when someone would make ignorant comments to me, like saying that my mom wasn't my "real mom." When my mom heard these kinds of comments, she would set that person straight as well. Like most kids who are adopted, when I was younger, there were times when I would try to use my adoption as an excuse, shouting at my mom, "You're not my real mom!" But I always knew deep down that I was a member of the family, and that my mom—even though she is not my biological mother—is still my mother.

Looking different from my family is not something I actively thought about when I was growing up. Most of the time, being adopted and looking different wasn't a big struggle or insecurity of mine, and when it was, I hid it well.

However, the appearance of my family mostly affected me when I was in elementary and middle school. I dreaded going with my parents (mostly my mom) to back-to-school functions. I never wanted either of my parents to go. Walking around and introducing my parents to my peers created the opportunity for those who didn't understand to ask stupid questions or to stare at us in confusion. After explaining that I was adopted, I used to tell others that I looked more like my father, because he had grey hair and I had black hair. Black hair was closer to my dad's grey hair than it was to my mom's light brown hair. Although I had insecurities around looking different, they never stopped me from attending those back-to-school functions. I would just cope as best I could until it was over and I could go home.

It's not that I felt embarrassed about being part of an adoptive family, it's just that I hated the questions that reflected so much curiosity and misunderstanding. I would get the Asian stereotype questions: "Did you get all A's on your report card?" "Are you good at piano or violin?" "Are you good at math or science?" I think I hated people asking those questions because not only were they singling me out because I looked different from them, but because deep down inside, I don't "feel" Asian. I was adopted by a white family, raised and brought up by a family whose background is Italian. I have never gotten all A's. I cannot draw to save my life. I honestly do not know how to read music notes, and math and science are so not my subjects. I am also a good driver (ha-ha). I think that people's questions were upsetting because they were reminders to me that I was "different."

As I grew older, I stopped worrying so much about how my family appeared in public. It's just become something that I don't pay attention to. I might notice and get annoyed if someone is staring too long, trying to make sense of the appearance of my family. But I generally am not as bothered now as when I was in elementary and middle school. It's not something that I really focus on.

I have never really given much thought to my birth parents or my birthplace. I think that teenagers who do struggle with not looking like their parents might question their identity. But for me, the struggle with identity came more into play in my later teenage years and into college.

I go to a "big ten" university, so it's a pretty big place, with the opportunity to always meet new people. I grew up in northern Virginia where I was exposed to people of different ethnicities. Coming to college, I experienced a profound culture shock. Although my school is big, diversity is lacking and stereotypes are very present. Most of the student body is Caucasian. Even though there is a large international student population with many students from China, I do not interact with them. The students from China generally do not speak English and keep to themselves. Being raised and brought up by a white family, I identify with being "more" white than I consider myself to be "Asian."

Nevertheless, I have had to deal with stereotypes and racism because I am Asian. I found this to be quite challenging when I tried to join a sorority. While I knew that rushing a sorority was likely to be a judgmental and shallow experience, I was not prepared for the stereotypes I encountered and the feeling that I was being compared only to the other non-Caucasian girls. I did not feel that I was being judged on my personality.

I think that going to school in the middle of Pennsylvania has opened my eyes to the fact that not everyone was fortunate like me to have been able to grow up in such a diverse area. I think growing up where I did, people are just more comfortable and familiar with a diversity of races other than white, and have better boundaries around what is acceptable to say and what is not. I have experienced a great deal of misunderstanding about being adopted here at school. At home in northern Virginia, it's just not a big deal—much more "normal" that someone might be adopted from a different country.

I try not to let ignorant people and their comments get to me, but every now and then, I do sometimes have to explain to people that I was raised in a Caucasian family, not the traditional Chinese one that people expect. Fortunately, my mom has always been very open to meeting new people, including those from different backgrounds. I think that her openness and willingness to expose herself to people who look physically different and come from different walks of life has helped me to be more tolerant of the different people I have encountered at school.

From my experience going to school in the middle of Pennsylvania, I know that growing up in a diverse area has significantly impacted how I feel about adoption. Because of the experiences at college, I sometimes wonder if I would feel differently about being adopted and Asian if I had grown up in a less diverse area. Would I be more curious about my birthplace or family? Would I have more interest in seeing or learning about the country I was born in? Everyone accepts and deals with their adoption differently; no one way is right.

Emily

Ren, 21

For whatever reason you have decided to read this book, it can be concluded that one reason specifically has drawn us all together. Adoption. Whatever your connection to adoption—you are an adoptee, adoptive parent, relative, friend—whatever the reason may be, my hope is that you find the satisfaction you are seeking somewhere in this compilation of personal experiences. My voice alone may not be much, but a combination of them holds considerable potential to be extremely powerful.

My name is Ren and I am 21 years old. I was a week shy of three when I was adopted from Yangzhou, Jiangsu, China and brought over to complete my forever family. Everything prior to the orphanage is basically blank space on my timeline. My birth parents left no information of any sort when they abandoned me. I do not hesitate to acknowledge adoption as the main source of emotional turmoil I have experienced throughout the roller coaster ride of life. Yet, at the same time, it is because of this background that I have become who I am today. But before I proceed, let me make one thing clear. Every person finds his/her own way to cope with adoption and even those methods are prone to change with time.

As a young girl, I was very timid, extremely soft-spoken, and disliked attention of any sort. I connected those traits back to my days in the orphanage where I was among many children who were only spoken to and not encouraged to speak up. Listen and follow, listen and follow. It took many years for me to gain enough confidence to be able to do most things on my own without feeling the need to look to someone for reassurance. I have found much comfort in connecting with other adoptees who are also interested in learning more about adoption. In addition, art has become a huge escape when it comes to expressing emotions I may not necessarily wish to say out loud. As I reflect, I realize that I am now quite outspoken about my adoption story. Although adoption does not define me, it is a part of me.

My lesbian parents adopted my sister, also from China, two years before I joined the family. The birth dates given to my family by our respective

28

orphanages indicated that I was only four months older than my sister. Because China prefers older prospective adoptive parents, my parents were in their mid-forties when they adopted my sister and me. One could argue that each family is "different" in its own way but when compared to the traditional "ideal" American family, my own family was especially different on many levels. Being someone who is exceedingly self-conscious, being adopted, not looking like my parents, and having two mothers, created much discomfort for me while growing up.

My family finds much humor in the fact that the only blood related living beings in our household are our two cats who came from the same litter. My sister and I find it quite easy to confuse people. Same race, same grade, same age, same last name but not twins? Some people will insist that we look alike, while others will see no similarity at all. Having a sister who was not only adopted, but also practically the same age as myself, made living as an adoptee easier to cope with. I always had one person I could confide in. Being a "different" family made my sister feel self-conscious as well. We were careful about whom we shared our story with and rarely invited friends to our house unless we knew them well. On a more positive note, whenever we were in public and one of our mothers was embarrassing us, it was easy for my sister and I to walk away and pretend we had no relationship whatsoever to the crazy Caucasian lady in the checkout aisle who managed to spill the orzo everywhere!

Both my mothers where born and raised in the Midwest. We often visited relatives living in places with little diversity and that were predominantly Caucasian. It was during those visits when I was keenly aware of being a different race than my parents. One memorable incident happened while visiting my grandmother in Michigan. During the summer, the local high school would rent their auditorium to artists. One summer, signs advertising Japanese sister duo pianists were placed all around town. My mother told me that one day, while she was standing outside a shop as my sister and I were inside exploring its treasures, she overheard a passerby remark to another, "Oh, those two girls in there must be the pianists here to perform in a few days." A few days later, when my family went to the performance, people at the front counter asked if my sister and I were the pianists. After the show, the two pianists were in the lobby to sell their CDs. My sister and I asked them to take a photo with us. I remember that as I was smiling for the camera, I realized that people in the lobby had become quiet and were just staring at us. It was so uncomfortable.

It was only at the end of my senior year of high school that gay marriage was legalized in the United States. My sister and I attended small private schools all throughout lower, middle and upper school. In elementary school, people were more aware that I have two mothers than they were after that. My sister and I were very private about that fact. During my first year of high school, the only openly gay person was cyberbullied. Sadly, that incident reinforced our fear of exposing that part of our lives to others. Even though I wanted to believe that most people wouldn't judge me or change their opinion about me after learning about my two moms, I never could be comfortable with testing that assumption.

While my family is "different" from the "average," none of those factors mean I am any less than anyone else. Family is family and I have recognized my own as it has been and will always be. There is nothing I can do to change the facts and as I have matured, I have reached a place of peace with that truth. In a way, I attribute a large part of my current well-rounded character to all those years of coping with having my "differences" probed from all directions. My advice to others: be proud of who you are and your family, and do not let other people hurt your self-esteem or self-confidence.

Amnoni, 29

My name is Amnoni and I am 29 years old, and my birth and adoptive families are African-American. Most of my childhood was spent in foster care. After being adopted and having "permanency" at age 15, I always felt robbed of the opportunity to be raised by my own parents. I felt that I did not have a natural support system to help aid in my success. I grew up with the idea that I could not achieve much in life because I was constantly reminded of my birth parents' mistakes and failures. I did not have the opportunities that most young people have to explore who they are within their biological family system. Instead, I grew up with a sense of not knowing who I was because statistics and stereotypes dictated my life. I did not have the space to question or explore who I was as an individual because throughout my life, I was focused on my survival.

I knew that I was different from a very young age; I did not fit into "the box," nor was I the typical standard. My life was not traditional, but I was not allowed to be anything different from what I was taught to be. I grew up as a Christian in a fairly conservative household, and there were expectations placed on me from the beginning of my life. Because my identity was shaped through this lens—exploration, questioning the norms, and having the ability to fully engage with who I was were out of the question.

One afternoon, when I was 24, I sat in my therapist's office frustrated and overwhelmed with everything happening in my life. Dealing with years of trauma, the effects of childhood sexual abuse, and lifelong abandonment were issues I was constantly working through. Deep down inside, I was frustrated because I was afraid and ashamed of what I was about to share with my therapist. But I knew that today was the day I needed to finally share this. These feelings were something I could no longer shake off or hide behind, despite years of suppression and shame.

My therapist finally asked, "Kiddo, how are you doing?" I did not know how to put it all into words, but I began listing several stressful things I was experiencing at the time. I then paused (hoping I would forget), and finally said, "And on top of all of this, I THINK I'M GAY!" My voice shook as I was nervously waiting for her response. I was waiting for her to squirm, make weird faces, or be disgusted with what I just told her. To my surprise, she said, "Oh, sweetie, you're normal, and that's ok!" I was relieved because repeatedly, no matter what I shared with her, she always normalized my experiences and feelings. Hearing her say those words was so impactful because I grew up in an environment where I had to be perfect, my feelings weren't normal, and I was not allowed to question anything. I already felt different since I did not grow up with my biological parents, because being different felt so wrong, because I was not always aware of who I was, what was right or what was acceptable.

As my therapist and I continued to talk she encouraged me to begin exploring my sexuality because it was an important step in getting to know that part of myself. *"ARE YOU KIDDING ME??!"* I exclaimed. *"I can't explore that. That goes against my beliefs as a Christian."* I was trying to put myself deeper in the closet, while she was trying to bring me out. If I'm honest, I was deeply afraid of abandonment and rejection. I was also very nervous about how people would view and treat me if they knew the truth. Growing up the way I did, abandonment and rejection was my norm, so I was afraid of coming out because of the fear of being rejected yet again.

For years I had struggled with my sexual identity, and each night I would pray and beg God to erase my "sinful" feelings of liking women. I thought I was an abomination because I was attracted to something other than what I thought I was created to be attracted to. I dated men just so I could prove to myself that I was straight, and I was constantly in a state of depression because I blamed myself for not being able to fit into the norm of heterosexuality.

As I thought about my therapist's suggestion of exploring, I was not sure what that entailed. I wondered if I would fail at it, or if it was better for me to play it safe. I finally took a risk. I started hanging with groups of people who were more affirming, attending LGBTQ events, and I joined a dating website. I enjoyed these experiences because I was beginning to challenge and question the very ideas and beliefs I'd been raised with that caused me to hate myself. I could not quite understand how God could love me unconditionally, but stop loving me because I couldn't help who I loved. I had been living under the impression that I could not reconcile this conflict, but these experiences taught me that I could.

Even though I was enjoying the freedom of exploration, I remained anxious about "being found out." I was afraid that someone would "out me" (call me out publicly for being gay) so I hid within spaces. My identity was often tied to other people. I cared more about what other people thought of me than what I thought of myself. Furthermore, I continued to not have permission to think and do for myself, and that reality often dictated my actions.

As time passed, my confidence grew as I explored my identity. I became increasingly unapologetic about who I was and cared less about what people thought of me. I realized that if I did not fully accept who I was, how could I expect others to? I started challenging myself to speak out about issues that are important to me, after remaining silent for years, fearing what others would think. This was an important step for me to take because I learned to stand up for myself and that my existence was important, no matter whom I loved.

On February 14, 2017, I publicly came out as Lesbian. I purposely chose Valentine's Day because it was an act of self-love. I also knew that for me to help liberate others, I first needed to liberate myself. I was tired of hiding, and I soon learned that if people were not going to accept me for who I was, then they did not need to have me in their lives. To my surprise, I had a pretty positive experience. People whom I expected to have a hard time with my sexual identity embraced me with no questions asked. Many others also came out to me and thanked me for inspiring them to do so. I never imagined that this would have been my experience, yet I am thankful.

At the same time, I did not expect to be rejected by my adoptive family, the people who claimed I was family for over 10 years. Because I could no longer be what they wanted for me, I was no longer relevant in their lives; I quickly became a stranger. Even though I lost people who were very important for me, I was determined to live my life according to my own standards and no one else's.

As I look back on my coming out experience, I recognize that learning about who I am is a lifelong process that will continually evolve, grow, and change. Thinking back to my sessions with my therapist, I am thankful for her leadership and role in my life because she gave me the courage and permission to explore. She gave me permission to be my true self and more importantly, she challenged me to take unbelievable risks. Each day I am learning that if I hold myself back from being all that I am, I stop myself from loving all of who I am.

Knowing who you are is truly important and necessary for your life's journey. The task of understanding oneself can often be complex, scary, and overwhelming. But what I've learned is that taking the risk to love myself, no matter what, is a true honor. Growing up, my identity was shaped on false beliefs, and standards that I was not able to identify with. Each day, I give myself permission to establish and define who I am; I set my own standards at my own pace, and I create the life I want, not the life I was given.

amor

Rachel, 34

In 1982, my biological mother was working as a dancer in a night club in Antofagasta, Chile. As she left work late one night, she was raped by a group of men. She was traumatized... afraid...and unbeknownst to her at the time, she was pregnant. My mother's attack not only left her pregnant with her second child at the young age of 19, but with a painful memory that she could not bear to have a permanent reminder of in the form of a child.

I was born in Santiago, Chile in July of 1983. I was relinquished immediately after birth and spent six weeks in private foster care until my Caucasian Jewish parents came to adopt me. I arrived in the United States in August of that same year and my life of being "different" began.

As an international transracial adoptee, I was always stuck in being different. I knew I was different when I looked into my dad's piercing green eyes... when I held my mother's fair-skinned hand...when I sat around tables at family gatherings and nobody looked like me. I had tan skin, deep brown eyes, black curly hair, and my body had a dusting of dark hair all over. I remember stealing my mom's razor as a child and shaving my entire body with the hope that I would look lighter...more like my parents. With excitement, I looked in the mirror and was deeply disappointed when I realized nothing had changed. I still wasn't white. I looked exactly the same, just without eyebrows.

Growing up as an adoptee, my childhood was everything that most kids wish for. I lived in a beautiful home, in a wonderful community, and attended some of the best schools in Maryland. I had many friends, was active in sports, and went on exciting family vacations. To the outside world, I had it all. In my heart, something was missing. I have vivid memories of crying my eyes out as I looked out my bedroom window up at the sky. Through my tears, I would try to sing the lyrics from Annie's famous song of life as an orphan. "Maybe far away or maybe real nearby...he may be pouring her coffee, she may be straightening his tie. Betcha they're good, why wouldn't they be? Their one mistake, was giving up me." Fantasizing about my biological parents got me through many lonely nights as a little girl.

I felt stuck in being different when people came up to me and spoke to me in Spanish because I had no idea how to reply since I only spoke English. In high school, I SO badly wanted one of the "100% Latina" shirts being handed out by the Hispanic club. No matter how far I stretched my arms, getting the guts to ask for a shirt was always out of my reach. Despite having 20/20 vision, I convinced my parents to get me blue contacts with no prescription. But even with fake blue eyes, I was too Spanish-looking to fit in with the white kids.

Feeling like such an outcast made me an anxious, depressed teenager. I felt isolated, sad and alone, which led me to wander down roads of unhealthy habits. I spent years abusing drugs and alcohol. I was part of a group of kids who I suspect felt as bad about themselves as I did, but our troubles were unspoken. We skipped school and spent long nights clouding our minds from our insecurities and discomfort. We filled our bodies with substances that hid our sorrows. Somehow this behavior provided me with a sense of comfort, a sense of belonging.

When I was 15 years old, I began seeing the most amazing psychotherapist. She helped me battle through my darkest days, and she encouraged me to challenge all my negative thoughts about being different. Why was being different such a bad thing? My therapist worked diligently with me for 10 years. She helped guide me to dig deep into my adopted soul and heal the wounds that being a transracial adoptee had inflicted.

I am now a 34-year-old married mother of four amazing children. I own a successful business and I have been sober for 10 years. I searched, found and reunited with my biological mother. I have a wonderful relationship with all my parents and for that, I am truly thankful. As I've grown up, I've realized that being different is not one of my weaknesses, but rather one of my greatest strengths. It allows me to add different perspectives to conversations as I share my experiences.

If there's one thing I could help people understand about being adopted, it's that adoption is not a one-time event. Adoption is a process. A process of soul searching, a process of soul finding, a process of understanding, and in my case, a process of finding peace in being different.

Activity: Find a Song

Feeling different or feeling like you don't fit in or belong is something that happens to many people, not just those who are in adoptive families. There are many artists whose music speaks to feeling different.

Find a song that you think represents the way you feel different in the world.

Allie is 14 years old. When she was adopted from Kazakhstan, she was 1.5 years old.

Journal Reflections on Your Song

Write down the name and artist of the song you chose.

SONG'S NAME _____

SONG'S ARTIST _____

Describe why you chose this song. Was there more than one song you were considering? Describe what makes you feel different. How do the ways you feel different have a positive or negative effect on you?

_____
_____
_____
_____
_____
_____
_____
_____
_____
_____
_____
_____
_____
_____
_____
_____
_____
_____
_____
_____
_____
_____
_____

Journal Reflections on Your Song

Journal...continued

Journal...continued

Exercise Use Your 5 Senses

Mindfulness is an easy way to manage or regulate your thoughts and feelings. You can practice mindfulness anytime, anywhere. Take a minute or two now to focus on your five senses and see for yourself. Try for at least three items for each sense.

1. **What can I HEAR?** (clock on the wall, car going by, music in the next room)
   _____
   _____
   _____

2. **What can I SEE?** (my bed, that book, a person nearby)
   _____
   _____
   _____

3. **What can I SMELL?** (dinner cooking, my shampoo, the dog)
   _____
   _____
   _____

4. **What can I FEEL?** (the pen in my hand, the floor under my feet, my phone in my pocket)
   _____
   _____
   _____

5. **What can I TASTE?** (the gum I'm chewing, a recent drink, what I had for lunch)
   _____
   _____
   _____

Missing or Difficult Information

"What do my birth parents look like?"

"I was left outside an orphanage. What's my real birthday, and why was I abandoned?"

"My birth mother wasn't sure who my birth father was."

"My birth mother may not be alive."

"Do I have any brothers or sisters?"

As teens make sense of their adoption stories, they are faced with the significant losses they have encountered. These losses involve being separated from birth family members, whether you once lived with them or even if you never met them. Maybe you have had to leave foster families, perhaps your birth country. You want to understand why you have experienced these losses and you likely have many questions about what happened to you and why. You want to fill in the missing pieces of your puzzle.

In your desire for information about your birth family, you may find yourself deeply frustrated by the lack of answers your parents are able to provide, either because they have so little information, or are trying to protect you from painful details. It is also possible that you DO have information that is really hard to accept—information that leaves you with serious feelings of sadness, anger, confusion, or anxiety. It is not uncommon to wonder and worry about what this information means about you and its implications for your life.

Anna, Tatyana, Skyler, and Leah share their stories of the impact of missing and/or difficult information on their lives and what they experienced when they could get answers to their questions.

Anna, aa

I was adopted from Russia when I was eight years old, a month shy of my ninth birthday. My birth mother was an alcoholic and due to severe neglect and lack of care, my brother and I were removed from our home and taken to an orphanage. My family was very poor and most of the money we did have was usually spent on alcohol and cigarettes. My mom would bring men home, and very often they would get blackout drunk and beat my mother. The images of my mom getting beaten always replay in my head and I have trouble remembering days when she was happy.

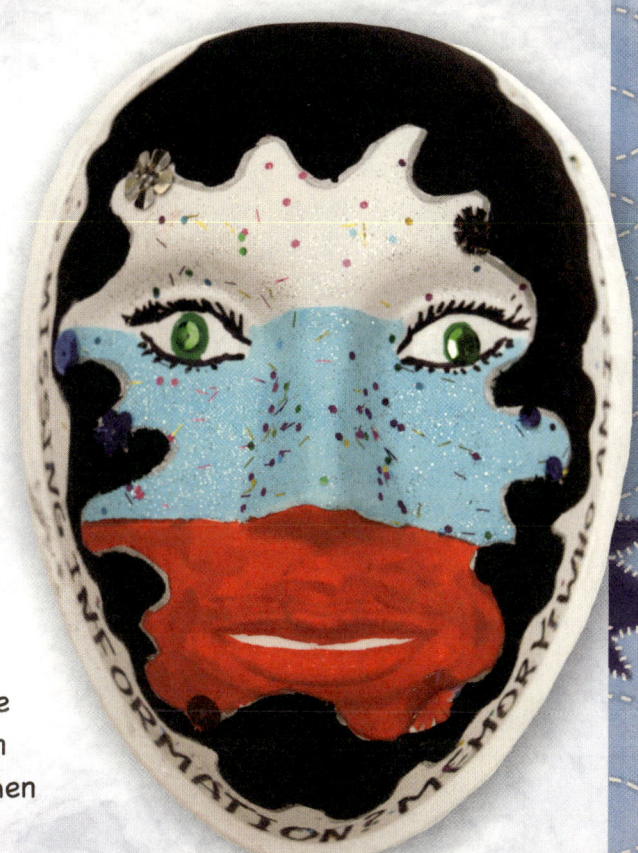

During the adoption process, I did not have much knowledge of what that entailed. I never imagined that I would never see my mom again. If I had understood, I would have remembered her eye and hair color, what she liked to do, her smile, the sound of her voice, the way it felt to hug her and everything else about her. I wonder if she thinks about me or misses me. I wonder if she still remembers me and our moments together, or even if she's still alive.

I was adopted into an older Caucasian family with two biological adult children. My siblings look just like my adoptive parents and I can only imagine who I look like in my birth family. I grew up believing my biological brother and I had the same birth father, but I later found out that we did not. Without information about my birth dad, I will probably never know what he looked like. When I go to the doctor and I am asked about my "family medical history," I am reminded that I do not know it. I don't know if I have any other family members other than the ones I know about. I don't know what diseases run in my family and I don't know what I will pass on to my own children.

The hardest part of being adopted is not knowing things that most people know about their families. I lived with my brother and my birth mother for five years before I was taken away by social services. I wish I could ask my mother why she had to leave me alone that morning or why I did not get to say goodbye to her. I wish she would have known what was going to happen so maybe it could have been less scary for me. I want to know my birth parents' past. I wonder if I ever meant anything to my birth father or if he even knows that I exist. The stuck spot of missing information really hits home for me.

When I went to C.A.S.E. for counseling at age 13, I was really struggling with all the issues I have mentioned above. I would cry all night long because I did not understand why I had to leave my family. I did not understand that my mother had a problem, and that she had been warned that the day would come when our family would be torn apart.

I did not know anything about the severity of my life in Russia because from my perspective, the way I had been living was just like how everyone lived everywhere in the world. In Russia, I had no guidance. In my village, as kids, we just took care of ourselves and did all we could to survive. My brother and I had to find food for ourselves by going to a local dump. Some days there would be barely anything to eat, so we would steal from nearby farms or beg our friends for anything they could spare. When I came to America, that need for survival continued. Because I missed the connection I had with my mother, I acted out by stealing and lying. The stealing was chronic and if I had not changed my ways with the help of my therapist, I would probably have ended up in a juvenile detention center.

In counseling and with my adoptive parents, it was hard for me to open up because of the lack of connection I felt toward my adoptive parents. My therapist would always tell me that it was normal for children with my experiences to act out and that I was not the only one. She would guide me in learning new ways to communicate with my adoptive parents about my pain, but it took a long time for me to respect their emotions and their struggles with me. Since my way of dealing with pain was through lying and stealing, my parents were not able to trust me for a very long time. Even as I grew older and began to really change my behavior, it was still hard for them to trust me.

It was extremely helpful to me to see that my therapist was always in my corner, standing up for me and trying to help my parents understand me. A therapist knows that adopted kids are hurting deep inside, in ways most people do not understand, and they can help guide conversations between teens and their parents. Over time, I was able to sit with my parents and talk about my feelings. My lying began to diminish and my parents started trusting me. In return, the feelings of aloneness and disconnect between me and my adoptive parents began to vanish.

When I turned 18, my mom created a book containing all the U.S. and Russian adoption agency records that my parents had regarding my adoption. I read the court documents and I learned my birth mother's middle name and my birth father's name. As I continue to get older and face new experiences, my past follows me. It makes me who I am. I know that if I had not received help from C.A.S.E. when I did, I would have gone down a dark path. Though it still hurts not knowing answers to my many questions, I have come to a place of acceptance and peace. One day, from the information I have in my possession, I will track down my birth mother to find the missing pieces to the puzzle of my past.

Anna

Tatyana, 19

My name is Tatyana, or Tati, as my friends like to call me. I am 19 years old. I was born in Russia and adopted a month after my seventh birthday. My Caucasian adoptive parents had a biological child, but due to medical problems, my mom was unable to become pregnant again. They chose to adopt and found my photo on an adoption website. They came to visit me in the Russian orphanage where I lived in January 2005, when I was six years old, and again in May of that year. After all the paperwork was finished, I arrived home on May 18, 2005, when I was seven years old.

I chose to write about the stuck spot MISSING INFORMATION because that is the issue I have been struggling with most of my life. You definitely can't complete a jigsaw puzzle if some of the pieces are missing. It is also much harder if you don't have the picture on the box to guide you. Since I was older when I was adopted, I did have more of the pieces of the puzzle than many adopted kids have. I knew more about my story, but my memories were often vague and confusing, and I wasn't sure WHERE to put them.

Because of missing and incorrect information about my adoption story, after being adopted, I felt lost for a large part of my childhood. I felt like I didn't fit in. I felt sad, confused, angry, and just lost. I felt that my parents just didn't understand what I was going through, and I felt very afraid to trust them. I think because I felt this way, I built a big brick wall around myself and kept my true feelings to myself so no one could hurt me. I believed my birth parents must not have loved me or that I was a mistake because they weren't married when I was born. I wondered if the reason they relinquished me was because something was wrong with me.

Much of this confusion and pain had to do with the fact that when I joined my family, I didn't speak English and it was hard for me to understand what was happening. I was removed from my birth mother's care at four years old because of neglect, and I lived in the orphanage for three years with my half-brother, Oleg, who was five years older than me. When my adoptive parents came to get me, I wasn't given a chance to say goodbye to Oleg. Once I could understand English and communicate with my parents, they told me that the orphanage had lied to them by minimizing my bond with my brother, claiming that we were half-siblings and not close at all. The pain and grief I felt about this loss made it harder to deal with the many other losses I was experiencing...loss of my home, my language, my culture, and my orphanage "family."

As I was trying to adjust to my new life, many questions were swirling through my brain. I opened up a little and told my parents what I remembered about my birth family. I wondered whether my birth parents were alive, where my brother was, and if he knew what had happened to me. I had an early memory of a house fire, wondered how and who started it, and feared my birth mom died in this fire. The only information my parents supposedly had was about my brother, and the fact that no one (birth parents, relatives) had come to visit me in the orphanage.

When I was about 10 or 11 years old, I found my adoption papers. I found something that at first looked like a birth certificate, but attached was a translated version that said DEATH CERTIFICATE in bold letters. It was my birth mother's death certificate. I ran to my room and cried for hours, feeling even more broken and confused inside, but I didn't tell my parents until years later. Instead, I began acting out, stealing little things from stores that my parents refused to buy for me, like candy and makeup. That lasted for about four or five years. Besides stealing, I was often reckless. When I was 12, a friend and I were playing with matches. We accidentally started a fire in the woods, and the police came. I ran, but the police came to my house. I was lucky that I only received a warning, but I was really scared, and told myself I had to stop.

My parents wanted to help me and to understand what I was going through, so we started counseling. We tried group and individual therapy, but I wasn't opening up. I participated in a grief group in my middle school, and for the first time, I realized there were other kids struggling with similar challenges. The school referred me to a program for adopted middle schoolers and I began seeing a therapist who specialized in adoption. I have been seeing her for six years, and I must say that I am a totally different person from who I was before I met her. She was also adopted and I feel that she has always understood what I am going through. I have always felt that I could tell her what I was thinking and feeling.

During these years, I still had problems fitting in, but I think my family and therapist helped me the most. I worried about the bad things I did and if my adoptive parents would give up on me. When I was going through the stealing phase, my grandmother on my dad's side told me she would always be there for me, no matter what I did. She told me I could always talk to her and that no matter what, I would always be her little princess. She told me that she would love me even though I made mistakes. It helped me to remember her words whenever I felt really scared of being given away again.

As I continued to go to therapy, I was able to slowly open up. My therapist gave me tips on how to deal with my thoughts and feelings. When I went to see her, I didn't feel like it was a therapy session. We played games, and it felt like we were just having a conversation.

During high school, many difficult feelings came up for me that were mostly related to all the unanswered questions about my family and my past: *Where was my brother and was he OK? What happened with the fire? What exactly happened to my birth mom? And my birth dad?* I remember getting into a fight with my adoptive mother. I don't remember what it was about or how it started, but I will always remember the words she said:

"*She is gone. I am your mother. Put the past behind you and move on.*"

I know she meant well and was just trying to help me get better. I know she didn't understand how much that hurt to hear. I was able to talk about what happened in therapy, and my therapist helped my parents understand how deeply those words (although true) affected me, triggering my unresolved grief. She helped them understand how the missing information about my story (what I DIDN'T know) made it even more complicated and emotional.

Two years ago, I discovered a Russian website like Facebook. I found a guy with my brother's name who looked like him. I messaged him, and received a reply saying he WAS my brother. I went behind my parents' backs to do this, and when I told them, they were NOT happy. They were not opposed to the idea of searching; they just wanted to be involved. They wanted to slow down the process to make sure I was prepared for what I might learn, and protect me from information I might not be ready to deal with.

And they were right. I was not ready for some of the information that I learned. Or at least not so fast. I rushed into asking lots of questions, and got lots of answers, and it was overwhelming. Other birth relatives started reaching out to me, and two days before my 18th birthday, my birth aunt sent me a picture of my birth mother's grave. In addition to learning missing information, I learned that some of the information I believed to be true was not.

Some of what I learned was a relief, and some details were hard to hear. I learned that the fire was no one's fault, and that it wasn't the cause of my birth mom's death. I always carried the feeling that no one must have cared about me from being told that no birth relatives visited me while I was in the orphanage. I was so relieved and happy to learn from my birth aunt that my birth mother loved me a great deal, but was unable to care for me because she was ill. I learned that my birth aunt made attempts to have me live with her, which were unsuccessful. I also learned that my birth father, who I thought was involved at least somewhat in my life, had never been involved at all.

Today, while there is still a lot to process, I am more at peace with my story and my history. I have always had a short temper and have noticed that since learning this information, I have better control over my emotions and don't blow up as fast.

If I had a message to share with other teens, I would say that learning the true details of your own history can be challenging, but they can also be grounding and stabilizing. Let others help you by talking to them about your questions, fears, and accomplishments, too. If your parents or professionals try to help you, let them, even if you would rather not! Remember, if you are hurting down deep, it will come out some way or another, and sometimes it comes out in ways, like lying and stealing, that just add to your problems.

I am currently preparing to participate in a 10-month AmeriCorps program, and have plans to attend college after I complete the program.

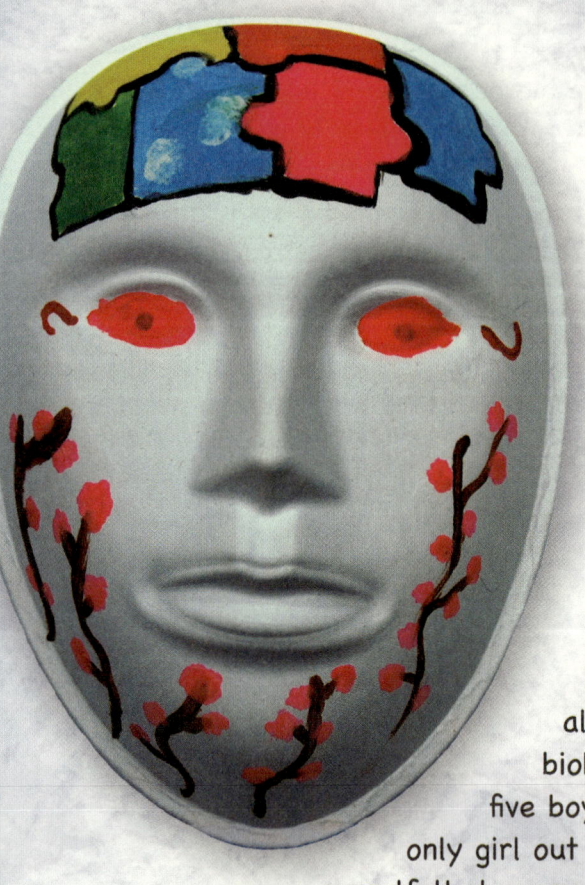

Skyler, 18

Hello, people reading all about me. I'm Skyler and I'm 18 years old and African-American. I was adopted by two wonderful, caring, strong Caucasian women that I call my beautiful mothers. I was adopted when I was two years old from foster care in Washington, D.C., along with my older brother Anthony, who is now 19. I live with my moms and five brothers, who were all adopted as well. Two of my brothers are my biological brothers. Yes, I am the only girl out of five boys. Yes, I know what you are thinking, "Dang, only girl out of five boys! How does she do it?" Yes, I ask myself that every day!

I was born in D.C. to a very poor family, living in a dark apartment building with many siblings as well as other kids and adults. Nothing to play with but the bugs that crawled on the cold floor. My birth mom was a drug addict and an alcoholic, and she was arrested for murdering a man for drugs. That is why my siblings and I went into foster care. After my birth mother's arrest, my moms learned about me and my older brother Anthony because they had already adopted my older brother Michael, who is now 23. I am happy they adopted me. I love my family through thick and thin, and I know they love me very much. I thank God for them every day!

Nevertheless, I feel that there are still a couple of missing pieces to my life's puzzle. I believe that those two missing pieces are: 1) the lack of information I have about myself, my birth mom and my birth family, and 2) my identity. When I was little, being adopted and not knowing about my birth mom never bothered me. I just knew that I was adopted and that I now felt safe and loved. But as I grew older, my mindset and my thoughts began to change and evolve into a wild world of questions and feelings I had never felt before. I wondered, *Why did my birth mom choose drugs and alcohol over me? Do I look like my mom? What does my mom even look like? What did I look like when I was born? How come all my friends have baby pictures and I don't? Did my birth mom love me? Does she even remember me?*

These questions in my head would go on endlessly. I would get upset, feeling that I was unwanted because everyone else had a mother who kept them and loved them, while mine chose drugs and alcohol over me. But am I ungrateful? I was blessed with a wonderful adoptive family, but I still wished that I knew my birth mom. I wondered if it was wrong to feel that way. All these questions and thoughts would stress me out. I didn't really like talking to my parents about this because I worried they would be sad that I felt this way. I was also not inclined to express my feelings to others because I believed doing so would make me look weak.

Another stuck spot that I would struggle with was my identity. I am proud to be African-American! But as I grew older, I realized that my family looked nothing like other families. Everywhere I looked I saw Caucasian parents with Caucasian children, African-American parents with African-American children, but my family was different: Caucasian parents with African-American children. We were different. Every time I made a new friend and they would meet my parents, they would always say, "Wait, that's your mom? She's white...were you adopted? What happened to your real parents? Why do you have two moms?"

I can't even begin to tell you how many times I've been asked these same questions. They always bothered me a little, as I wondered, *Are they trying to say that there is something wrong with being adopted?* In my heart, I knew there is nothing wrong with my family because I loved them and they loved me, but why did everyone always seem to feel bad for me and ask me the same questions when they found out I was adopted? It used to be mind-boggling, but now I know it's just that other people are curious and wanting to know about me because I'm not like them—my family is a little bit more unique.

Over the years, I have learned that there are many other adopted kids struggling with the same questions. When I was in middle school, I participated in a program with other adopted middle school kids. Being around so many others with similar stories and questions was extremely helpful to me. I could easily express my feelings about being adopted because I didn't feel judged.

Now that I am about to be a freshman in college, I do still occasionally struggle with these questions. When I'm a little older, I plan to find my birth mom and hopefully get answers to my questions. My main message for other adopted teens is that although you may be struggling to find your path in life, don't get discouraged. Stay strong and continue your journey to success and your path will find you. ✺

Leah, 13

Hi, my name is Leah. I am 13 years old, and in the seventh grade. I live in a Caucasian family, which consists of my mom, dad, and 19-year-old sister, who is the biological child of my parents.

I was adopted from China as an infant. Back then, China had a law stating that couples were only allowed to have one child due to the population growth. Additionally, most people preferred sons because the custom in China is that the son and his wife take care of his parents when they are old. If a couple had a daughter, and she married, the daughter would have to take care of her husband's parents, leaving her parents all alone. That's why so many more girls were abandoned and living in orphanages.

I was born in Guangzhou (Guangdong (Foshan) Province), and was found on a corner of an intersection right under a tree. I had enough shade, but not so much that I wouldn't be seen. People noticed me, and were telling everyone that there was a baby in a wooden crate under a tree. I was found by a woman who oversaw a government agency located in a building across the street, so I think I probably have smart birth parents because they chose a good place to leave me!

I was taken to an orphanage that was connected to a senior citizens' home and stayed there until I was about nine months old. That's when my parents adopted me because they were looking for a second child.

When I was younger, I never really thought much about my adoption, but I knew my adoption story was this:

My parents flew all the way across the ocean to China and adopted me. A story as simple as that.

I have grown up with a diverse group of amazing friends. They never judge me or anyone on their looks. They know I was adopted and they respect that. When I was a younger kid in elementary school, I don't think it ever bothered me that I was an Asian adoptee growing up in a Caucasian family.

I chose to write about the stuck spot MISSING INFORMATION because at some point in the last few years, I realized that I didn't really know very much about my story before I joined my family, and that there is a missing part in my system. It feels like someone took a huge chunk of me and separated it from me. Now that I am a teen, I think that identity can sometimes be a struggle. If someone asked me who I am, I would say that I am a Chinese-American teenager. I have no clue why I put Chinese first, but maybe it is related to trying to figure out the part of myself that is Chinese.

When I was growing up, as far back as I can remember, my parents always wanted to have conversations about adoption and discuss how I feel about being an adopted person. I remember feeling uneasy and trying to change the subject because I never felt comfortable, especially when I was younger. I didn't understand why I was so opposed to talking to them at the time, but now I think I am starting to understand. Thinking and talking about adoption made it more real, and not having answers to questions made it more complicated. I think I just didn't want to deal with that!

I started meeting with my therapist a few years ago. I was pretty resistant and it took a long time for me to open up, but I slowly did. Talking helped me open up to MYSELF about what I wanted to know, and has also made me feel a little more willing to talk to my parents, although it's still hard.

Besides therapy and support from my family, I have been getting together for many years with a group of girls my age who were also adopted from China. We have fun together, and almost never actually talk about adoption, our common bond. But our moms do! And once a year we go to a Chinese restaurant to celebrate the Chinese New Year. Also, for several years, I have been attending C.A.S.E.'s annual Kids' Adoption Network (KAN) conference for children and teens with my parents. At the conference, we DO talk about being adopted and it has made me realize that other adopted kids have similar questions, feelings, and experiences.

My parents have done the best they could to help me find out more about my background. They even hired someone to help search for my information. That is how I found out that I was left on a corner in a wooden box under a tree in front of a government building. That is a start, but I wish I knew more, and I hope to someday meet my birth family. If I do meet them, I know I will have many questions. I want to know why they gave me up, if I was given a birth name, and where I got my stubborn streak from?

My advice to adopted kids is to try opening up to your parents about your questions and worries, even if it's hard.

At the moment, my life is going well. I love soccer, drawing, and reading. Pandas are my favorite animal.

Leah

Activity   Puzzle Pieces

Using colored pencils or markers, write on the puzzle pieces what you know about your story and what is missing. Write the known pieces as statements and the missing information as questions. Use as many or as few pieces as you need. Any pieces left blank may represent questions you may have in the future.

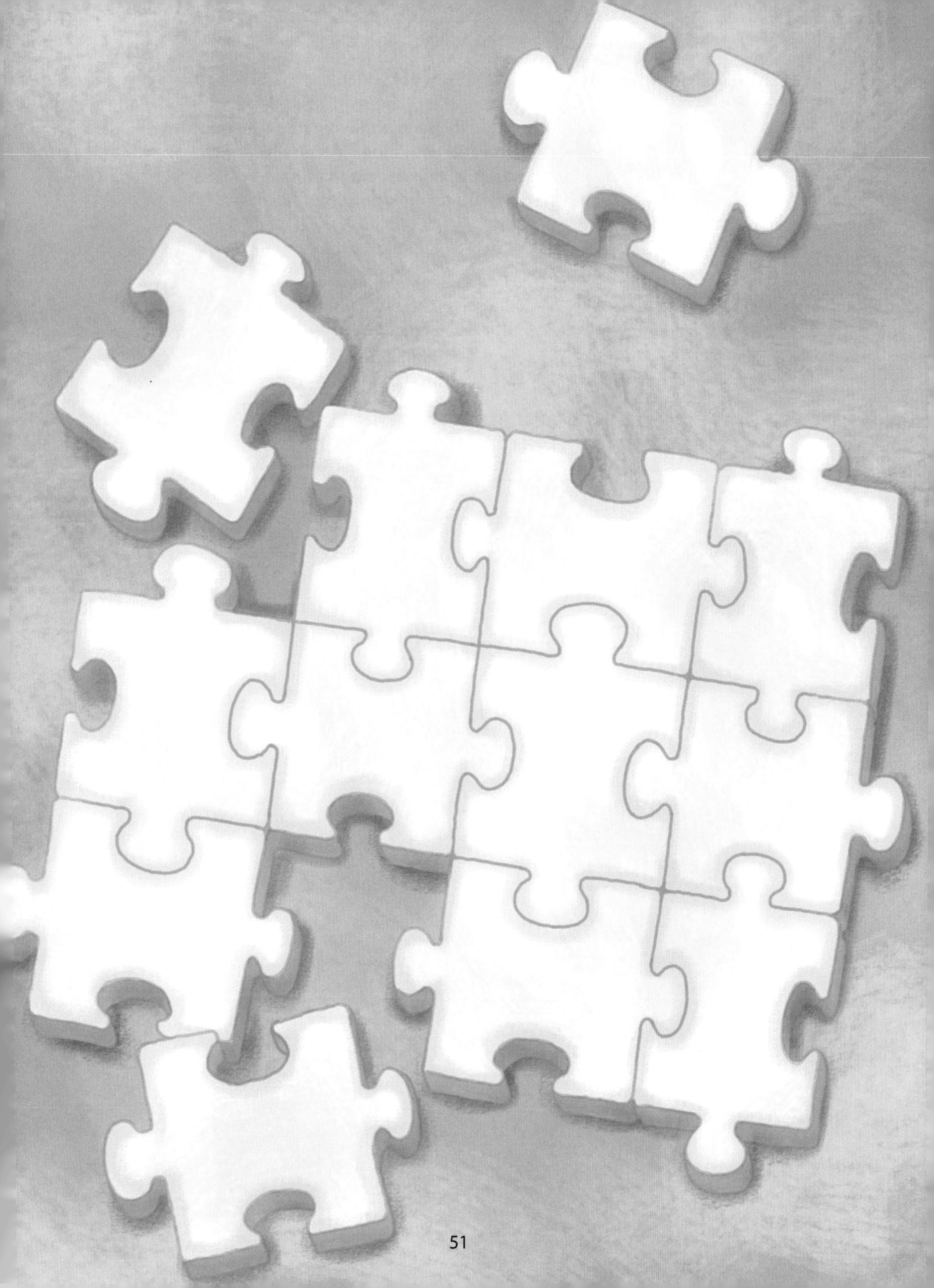

Journal What I Want to Know

What feelings do you notice when you are thinking about what you do or do not know about your story? How do you deal with those feelings? Who do you share them with? What do you hope the answers are to those questions that you have? What would be the most upsetting, painful, or difficult answers to those questions?

Journal...continued

Exercise: Relaxation Playlist

Use your favorite music platform to make a playlist of music that makes you feel happy, optimistic, and empowered. Listen to this when your thoughts or feelings are causing you to be upset.

Song _____

Artist _____

Song _____

Artist _____

Song _____

Artist _____

Song _____

Artist _____

Song _____

Artist _____

Song _____

Artist _____

Song _____

Artist _____

Song _____

Artist _____

Reason for Adoption

"Why was I given away? Was something wrong with me?"

"My birth parents used drugs, abused and/or neglected me; what does this mean about me?"

"Why couldn't my birth parents solve their problems and keep me?"

Like most adoptees, once you understood that adoption meant that your birth parents could not parent you, you began to think about the reasons "WHY" they did not raise you. Making sense of the reasons for your relinquishment is huge. Hopefully, when you were young, your parents tried their best to explain to you the circumstances surrounding your placement—in ways that children can understand. But honestly, it was likely very hard for you to understand. That is because adoption is always about ADULT DECISIONS and CIRCUMSTANCES that young children cannot comprehend. As teens, you are better able to understand what happened, but that doesn't mean you feel good about what you understand. Your sense of what happened can be extremely painful. You may feel angry, sad, confused, or any combination of difficult emotions.

In the following stories, Jake, David, Carrie, and Sara share their challenges to come to terms with their adoption stories.

Jake, 14

Hi, my name is Jake and I am 14 years old. I was adopted from Guatemala in 2004 when I was two months old. I live with my parents and older sister, who is not adopted.

I knew I was adopted from the beginning of my memory, but I didn't always know what it meant. To me, it was just like I had a word drawn on my forehead but didn't know what it said. I knew it was there, just never thought about what it meant.

I chose to write about REASON FOR ADOPTION as my stuck spot because one day I realized what adoption meant. It meant that your birth mother gave you away to be raised by other people. I got stuck in a slump of sadness and curiosity. You look at your parents, and realize that you're not related to the people you've spent your entire life with. You figure out that your "family" isn't really your biological family at all. And you begin to wonder who your real parents are and why you are with these people who aren't even related to you.

As I grew older, I tried not to care as much because I looked at the honest truth, which was that I am one of over seven billion people in this world, and there was the smallest chance that I would ever meet my birth family. However, my curiosity continued to grow. I would often cry when I was little, realizing that my family is out there somewhere in a big world and that I would never get to meet them. But growing older, I became more curious, eager to ask the millions of questions I had.

From what I understood, I was adopted from a family who lived in terrible poverty. I had two older brothers and by the time my sister and I were born, there just wasn't a way for my birth parents to take care of me.

During my time of sadness, my parents worked very hard to help me feel better. I would spend countless nights with them, discussing how I felt and why I felt the way I did. They answered the few questions that they knew the answers to. My parents decided to get me a therapist to help me with these issues. Therapy really helped me start to turn my sadness to acceptance about being adopted, and although I might never be able to meet my birth parents, I could try.

I am happy to share that I have, in fact, met my birth parents and was able to get answers to my many questions. I know this opportunity is one that many adopted kids never get to have, and I feel very fortunate. I learned that I am who I am because being adopted makes me unique, and in my case, being placed for adoption was for the benefit of my life. If it wasn't for my birth parents' decision to put me up for adoption, I would never be able to do all the things I do today. An example of something I wouldn't be able to do is practice my passion for Parkour and Freerunning. I have pursued this for many years and have become a Sponsored Athlete and Ambassador for Bolt Parkour and Freerunning Academy, which is a major accomplishment for me.

My advice for any kid who is adopted—stay positive and never lose hope about knowing where you came from. If it matters to you, you can try to find the information or the people you want to know. You'll never know if you don't at least try.

Jake

David, 12

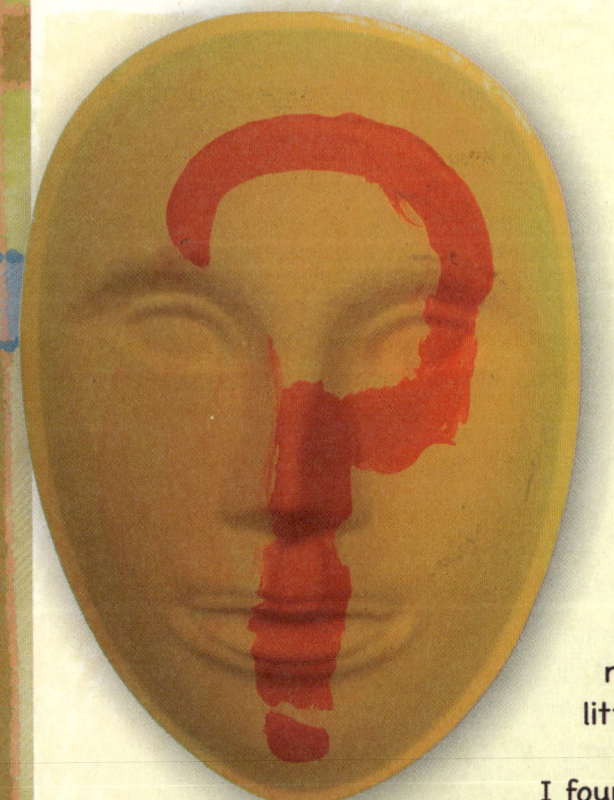

My name is David. I am African-American. I was adopted from foster care at the age of two by my parents who are from the Congo. At the age of eight, I was told the impossible. I was told that I was adopted. I couldn't believe a word of it. After all these years of hiding the truth, I was full of many feelings, but mostly frustration and sadness. I just wanted to know why. Why was I adopted? Over the next few years, my parents told me my story a little bit at a time.

I found out the reason I was adopted was because my birth parents were addicted to drugs. My birth mom left me in a store and the manager called the police. The police called social services and I was placed in foster care. I lived in two foster homes before I was adopted by my family, but I don't remember them.

My dad told me that the second foster home I lived in before my parents adopted me was nice. The family lived on a farm and there were three other foster boys living there. The reason I left the first foster home is unknown. I left the foster home on the farm to be adopted by my parents. At the time, my folks were also taking care of two other children whose parents were sick. Shortly after that, my birth sister, Mary, was born and she was placed with my family. Then my next sister, Elizabeth, was born and came to live with us, too.

I had a hard time when I found out the reason for my adoption. I felt depressed and mad that one little thing like a drug can do so much damage to so many people. I understand how drugs could have affected my birth mom's judgment, but I was still mad.

It took me almost a year to feel better after I learned my whole story. I saw two therapists at C.A.S.E., who helped me talk about my feelings and adjust to my story. When I first learned I was adopted, I was so upset that I ignored my parents and gave them the silent treatment. Therapy helped me to calm down. My therapists helped me to think about all the questions I had about my story and I came up with two whole pages of questions! They also helped me get the answers to my questions. And now I don't feel stuck because, for now, all my questions have been answered.

I am a sixth grader who loves basketball. I play for my community team. I like pizza and I love to play the game Fortnite.

I want adopted kids to know that you will be able to accept your story after a while, even if it is sad. Also, it's ok to keep your story private and not tell anyone who asks you about it unless you want to. Also, tell your parents how you feel, even if you are angry, because they can't help you unless they understand how you're really feeling.

David

Carrie, 30

My name is Carrie and I am a Taurus. I am an introvert and I am creative, candid, full of attitude and zeal for life. I have blonde hair and blue eyes. I love the beach, hot sauce, handstands and loud music. I was adopted because my birth parents were too young to raise me.

From a young age, I knew that I was adopted. I have two loving, devoted, understanding adoptive parents who did everything they could to explain it to me. I was told that my birth parents were in a relationship when my birth mother became pregnant just after graduating from high school. I have a photo of them together at their prom, which I can see when I close my eyes. I was told that my birth parents didn't stay together and that they wanted the best for me. I knew that my birth mother gave me away at the hospital and that I was in foster care for two weeks before I was placed with my adoptive parents.

That is the story I was told of how I suffered the greatest loss of my life. As I came screaming into this world, my birth mother was doing the hardest thing (I think I can assume that) she ever did, and I had nothing to do with it. I was just a little fetus kicking around inside an amniotic sac while my fate was decided. I could understand why I was adopted, but I didn't like it. I felt upset and sometimes angry at how seemingly stupid my birth parents had to be to get themselves into this situation, and that I had to be the one to suffer the consequences.

Growing up, I acted tough at school and in public. I didn't look like my parents and I had an arsenal of witty comebacks for people who pointed it out.

"Oh, where did you get that blonde hair!?" they would ask.

"It grew out of my head," I would say sarcastically with a cold glare.

My answers were met with discomfort and nervous laughter. Sometimes, I would simply say, "I was adopted," to stop people in their tracks. I wanted to make people feel bad for asking. I wanted everyone to feel as uncomfortable as I did. Every mention of my blonde hair and blue eyes is a reminder of why I should feel different. I did not like having to explain myself to others and I didn't see why I should have to.

As I grew older, I began to realize the weight of my birth mother's decision. At 18, I had a boyfriend and I was the same age as my birth mother was when I was conceived. No one was more terrified of getting pregnant than I was. I did not want to be in the position to have to make such a decision. Ever.

Bad choices. Mistakes. Risky behavior. These are words associated with teen pregnancy. I had many thoughts that were overwhelming. What did it mean about my birth mother that she got pregnant at 18? Was she ignorant, reckless, unlucky? Does she have regrets? What does that mean about me? Am I an overgrown mistake? A fun night turned disaster...? One thing for sure was that I was determined not to let what happened to her happen to me.

Several years later, I realized that it was up to me to forgive my birth parents and let go in order to move forward. Maybe they were stupid, maybe they were unlucky, but it doesn't really matter. I am here now and I must move forward.

Once I let myself feel the magnitude of being an unplanned pregnancy, of losing my birth mother, and of being different, I was able to let go of the feeling of unfairness. That's a lie. I still get stuck on the unfairness, but I am always working hard to acknowledge it and forgive it and let it go. I have stopped being obnoxious to people who are curious about me (for the most part) and started explaining my story with patience. I can acknowledge that I made it through a terribly traumatic event before I could even understand it, and I am who I am because of it. (And I like who I am.)

I have never reached out to my birth parents, but I plan to.

Carrie

I am made of longing, a fierce and graceful shout
And though I try to hold it in, my arms fly wild about
These things they try to chain me, but the key is in my hand
The fear of letting go recedes to seize a new command

– "Complete" by Ayla Nereo,
The Polish Ambassador, Mr. Lif

Sara, 30

I knew I was adopted from a very young age. In fact, I can't ever remember a time of not knowing that my two older brothers and I were all adopted. But I also learned at a very young age that my adoption was different from my brothers. I looked just like my adoptive mom. In fact, once a neighborhood kid accused me of lying when I told him I was adopted. And everywhere my mother and I went we were told how much we looked alike.

When I was four, my maternal grandfather passed away. As she was talking with me, my mother accidentally let it slip, "You know your grandfather took care of you when you were a baby."

Being the inquisitive child that I was I knew something didn't add up. How did the same grandfather—my grandfather—take care of me if I was adopted? How could he have known me when I was born? It was then that I knew, and I asked my mom point blank, "Am I related to you?" to which I meant by blood. She responded yes.

I didn't ask how I was related, and for years I wondered who my biological mother could be. For me, it was kind of a game. I'd imagine different scenarios in my head about why I was adopted and when people asked, I would tell them my birth mother was "probably a distant cousin or something." My parents would smirk, never sharing whether that was true or not.

When I would ask questions, I was told that when I turned 18, my biological mother would like to tell me the story herself, in her own words. Given that my two older brothers were also adopted, and that they had much less information than I did about their own birth parents, I accepted this without much protest.

I did wonder, however. Sometimes I feared that my biological mother would be something shameful or embarrassing—like she joined the circus and worked as a clown. But mostly, when I look back on that time, I'm struck by how little I thought about it and how little I cared. To me, I already had parents. Whoever these biological parents were, they weren't in the picture now. And I was fine with that.

When I was 17, still one year away from when I was supposed to learn my story, my mother took me to an Italian restaurant. It was there, over a plate of pasta, that she would tell me the truth about my adoption.

"It's Aunt Pam."

Aunt Pam? Immediately a wave of relief swept over me.

How could I have never put two and two together? How did I never realize that the person who adopted me was my own biological aunt? And the person I had always known to be my aunt? Well, that was my biological mom!

Now it dawned on me that not only was I related to my adoptive mother, but I had known my biological mother my whole life without ever realizing it.

I didn't learn the whole story that night, rather the details trickled out slowly over the next few years. Over time I learned that at the time of my birth, my birth mother was struggling with schizophrenia, homelessness, and alcoholism. She had spent most of her pregnancy in jail, which my mother believed saved me from being born with Fetal Alcohol Syndrome. My maternal grandfather was my primary caretaker. My crib was a cardboard box, and I lived in a motel room. When I was six months old, the woman I would grow up calling "mom," flew to California and returned home with me to Maryland to raise me with my dad.

Once or twice a year, I talk to my biological mother, whom I still call Aunt Pam even to this day. She told me that her alcoholism was the reason why she was not able to provide for me, with the implication that I should be leery of drinking as well. Because of her schizophrenia, she is unable to work and is taken care of by her husband. My birth mother is a woman of few words...a born-again Christian who has been sober for many years. I couldn't be more different. I was raised Jewish and I am politically active for liberal Democratic causes. Yet, despite our differences, there is no doubt in my mind that I am loved.

The details about my biological father continued to be hidden from me for many years. The truth is I was less interested in learning his side of the story. I have a very close relationship with my adoptive father, and always assumed that my birth father had probably abandoned me when I was young and played a small part in my life. For years, all I knew about him was that his name was Michael and he was a Dodgers fan. It would be ten years after I learned the truth about Aunt Pam, now in my late 20s, when again over a plate of pasta, my mother decided to tell me about my biological father.

My birth was very traumatic; I was being choked by my umbilical cord and was born via an emergency cesarean. But that's not the only reason my birth was so chaotic. The man my birth mother was dating at the time of my birth was African-American. But when I was born, it became clear to everyone in the room that he was not my biological father. So, who then was?

My mother told me that my biological father not only didn't abandon me, but had never even been informed that I was born. "Pam was too embarrassed," my mom explained. My biological father died of cancer never knowing that I existed.

Over the years, like many adoptees, I have struggled with the reason for my adoption. Because I hadn't known that my birth mother was unable to care for me, there were times when I wondered if she had ever loved me. This was especially difficult because I knew that I was related to her. Sometimes it felt like a cruel joke that everyone else got to know my story before I did. And because I didn't know that my birth father never knew about me, there were times when I wondered if he had deserted me.

Learning the reasons for my adoption—addiction, mental illness, homelessness—answered one big question and created a hundred more. For years I wondered if I would become an alcoholic or schizophrenic like my birth mother. And in my late 20s, I suffered a sense of loss when I learned that I would never have the chance to meet my biological father, and that he died never knowing that somewhere in the world, there was a little girl—now a woman—that he helped bring into this world.

As I have grown older, I have been better able to understand the gravity of my birth mother's situation. I am struck with how selfless she was in giving me up for adoption. She could have insisted on keeping me, putting me and my future at great risk. But she didn't. She chose to give me up to a loving family that accepted me with open arms. Even though my adoptive parents' marriage would fall apart and they would eventually divorce, my birth mother still believes to this day that giving me up was the right decision.

Now 30, I realize that my adoption was the greatest gift I've ever been given. The gift of love, a second chance at life. It remains the single most loving and selfless gift I can imagine. And for that I will always be grateful.

I do hope that if you are part of a kinship adoption, that you know the truth about how you are related to your birth parents. If you don't and are confused, show my story to your parents. It may help them understand that if they think they are protecting you by not sharing the truth, they are not. While the truth may be challenging, it can be healing and prevent unnecessary pain.

Sara

Activity: Finding the Words Puzzle

Hidden in the puzzle below are words from the previous stories that may spark some of your own questions. Search, find and circle them.

```
I A U U N I Q U E M R O B K T Y G Z C N
B M C J L A U W R Y A Y H C Y A O P V W
V T O N O I S I C E D N K I W K O O J A
A X B H Y R T G T Q O E H S E C J E G G
D E T A R T S U R F P N S R X B V O N I
B W T C Q V I B L E T T M S H T U R T F
K U W W S N G S L J I U S F E G T G F Y
I P K R Y N R Q O Y O A S Y E R O Z G A
R F E E L I N G S I N O P A Y P P O J A
S X O D H V S A X G R P S D W A Y E D C
K E W S N Q S S G O A U C G R X Y Q D C
K Z Y B M T J Q E H H G C E Z K M X Q E
D J F D O A T B Q N Q Z N I G K Q I F P
V R J R C F K W X X D T H R R D X S I T
H K Y D O O Y I B R S A S N Z X Z K M B
V W Z U V X L D R M A T S I P A R E H T
S J O Q U E S T I O N S F J L F D I L C
C X P Z X N W K Y K L L G N W O N K N U
I S R E W S N A E R C M F G O E I J Z O
Q P E V I T I S O P L R E T S O F B M K
```

Parents	Answers	Frustrated	Story	Depressed	Foster
Sadness	Curiosity	Accept	Unknown	Feelings	Adoption
Truth	Happy	Positive	Sick	Therapist	Decision
Questions	Unique	Try			

Journal: Letter to Your Birth Parents

Draft a letter to your birth parents. What would you want to know about them? What do you want them to know about you? What questions do you want answers to? Use the words from the previous word search to help guide what you say or ask. Remember you are writing this in your journal. It doesn't have to go anywhere or be seen by anybody else if that's what you choose. Or, you may want to share your letter. Think about sharing it with your parents or a therapist.

Journal...continued

Exercise Safe Space

Get comfortable where you are, uncross
your arms and legs, and relax.

Take a moment to notice your breathing.

When you are ready, imagine you are in front of a door. On the outside of the door, where you are, are all the things that are on your mind—worrying you, bothering you, or upsetting you. On the other side of the door is your own Safe Space. Imagine you are opening the door and stepping into the place where you feel completely calm, completely happy, and completely safe.

Shut the door behind you. All your worry, stress, and upset are shut out. No one can come into your Safe Space unless you invite them.

Look around. What do you see? What do you hear? What can you smell? Feel? Taste? Your Safe Space can be inside or outside, anywhere in the world or in the universe. It can be a place you have been to many times, a place you have read about, or a place you are creating now in your imagination.

Take a moment to explore your Safe Space. Notice how good it feels to be here. Stay as long as you like.

When you are ready, step back outside the door, knowing you can return whenever you like. In fact, the more you practice, the easier it will be to get to this Safe Space and that good feeling that comes with it.

> **BONUS:** For those of you who enjoy art, you may want to try painting, drawing, or making a collage of your Safe Space.

Loyalty

"I'll upset my adoptive parents if I ask too many questions about my birth parents."

"Things were bad in my birth family, but I love my mom and grandmother and still want to see them. If I love my birth family, how can I also love my adoptive parents?"

"I worry about my siblings who are in different placements."

Many teens experience tremendous guilt over their frequent and intense thoughts and feelings about their birth parents. Maybe you are afraid that if your parents knew how you felt about your birth family, they would be hurt, or disapprove, or worse, reject you. Especially if you have or had relationships with your birth parents, maybe you have worried that if you allow yourself to love your adoptive parents, you are being disloyal to your birth family. You may find yourself in this terrible place of not feeling like you have permission to love both sets of families. Perhaps it is difficult for you to acknowledge the positive ways you identify with both sets of parents. You may be keeping these thoughts to yourself and feeling very much alone.

Anna, Daniel, and Zoe share their stories of loyalty conflicts regarding their birth and adoptive families.

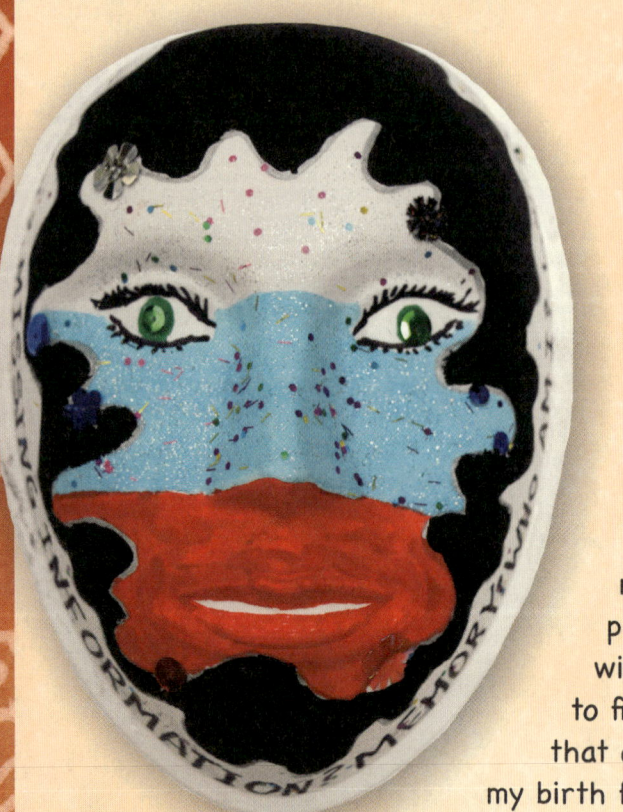

Anna, aa

(See Anna's essay under Missing Information, page 41, for her adoption story.)

Loyalty was never an issue for me until I became a teenager and started middle school. At that time in my life, I began to steal electronics and small things from other people as I began to question my adoption. I never had a problem with calling my adoptive parents "mom" and "dad" but I always had an issue with feeling like I belonged. Emotionally, I started to figure out that we were not really related, and that our lives and cultures were very different. With my birth family, I lived my life not knowing where my next meal would come from, not having any structure, and not having to answer to a parent. I came into a family that worked hard, and everything that I needed was given to me immediately. I did not know if I was "good enough" to be with my adoptive family because I had gone through so much and I believed that I was damaged.

My birth mom and I had a connection just like any child has with their mother. I knew her, I remembered our time together, and I remembered trying to be her protector. Even though it was not perfect or ideal, she was still my mother, and I loved and admired her like she was the most amazing woman in the world…and I still do. Because we have such different personalities, my adoptive mom and I never really clicked until I turned about 19 or 20. Occasionally, I wondered if my birth mom would be mad that I called my adoptive parents "mom and dad." Since I did not know my birth father, I wondered if he would care that I was bonding with another father figure or if he was happy that I was gone. There were also many questions in my early teenage years about whether my adoptive family was here to stay.

Beginning counseling helped me to learn how to deal with my emotions and how my adoptive parents were struggling just as much as I was. I remember many nights when I would scream into my pillow, "I WANT YOU, MOMMY!" or "WHERE ARE YOU?" because I was so angry and confused about who was my parent. I struggled and spent a lot of time crying because I could not share my real feelings for fear of hurting my adoptive parents' feelings. There were many times when I said, "I hate you!" to my adoptive parents because I wanted to hold on to that connection with my birth mom and deny that I was starting to feel like I had a real family. I had much to learn about my adoptive family so that I could understand where they were coming from, but I also had to learn to open up to my parents about my life so that they could understand why I acted the way I did and where I came from.

I think adoptive parents should always remember to never give up on their children when their children say they hate them. Their children do not mean what they are saying. The children are really feeling afraid, confused, and torn. I didn't really think about the impact of my words on my parents, but after I said hurtful things, I would calm down and write little notes of apology to them. When you are a teenager, pride can get in the way. Facing any person, especially your parents, and admitting you were wrong can be really hard. If communication is tough, as it was in my family, writing may help you to express your feelings as it helped me.

With the help of my counselor, I was able to understand that my loyalty to my birth mom is okay and it does not mean I love my adoptive parents any less. The yearning I always had to find my birth mother frightened me because I was afraid to hurt my parents' feelings. Being able to talk about this conflict in a safe environment helped me to understand that my parents wanted me to keep the connection with my birth mother just as much as I did. This stuck spot goes back to my stuck spot of missing information. Since I did not know much about my birth mother and my life with her, I desperately wanted to hold on to and preserve what I did know.

My parents have always been open to sharing their life stories with me and I was usually okay with giving them glimpses into mine. In counseling, conversations with my parents helped me to build my trust in them. My parents helped me to feel safe, and they let me know that they were trying their best. Instead of believing they were mean and evil after every fight, our counselor helped us to understand and interpret the true meaning of our feelings.

I learned over time that I can love my birth mom and my biological brother just as much as my adoptive parents and siblings, and I do not have to feel scared of being rejected by my adoptive family. I think that out of all the lessons I have learned, being able to appreciate my past has truly helped me to heal. I do not dwell in misery and sadness, and I am proud of how far I have come! Through my growth and success, my counselor made a huge impact on me by being one of my biggest supporters. As my confidence and strength grew, which was also a result of becoming more mature and learning from experiences, my parents grew as well. Together we learned to respect each other's struggles.

I know this book is for teens, but parents should read my story, too. This advice is for them: Parents need to remain supportive and encouraging. No matter how a child acts out, they should never make their child feel that they are "the problem." Instead, parents should try to understand that their child's problems are created from the child's past experiences.

Anna

Daniel, 20

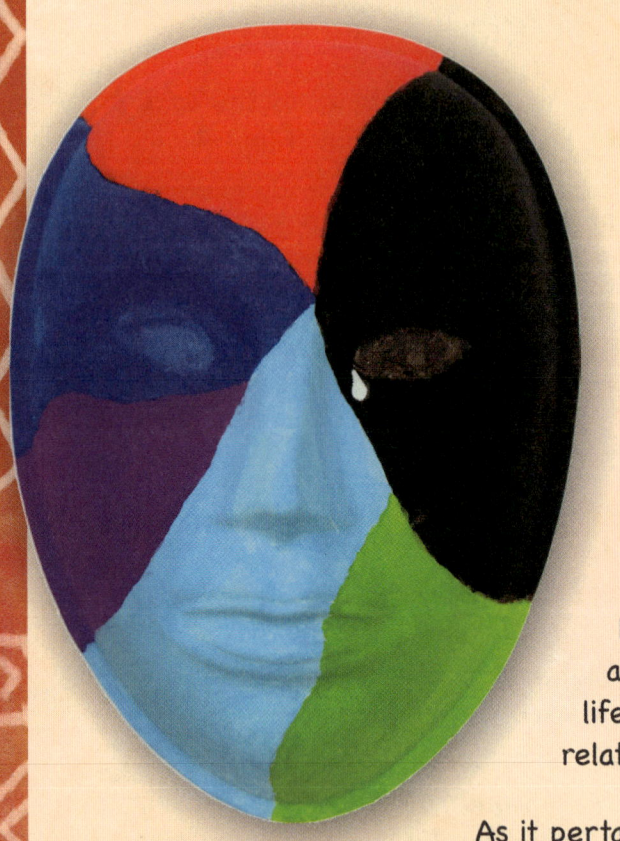

(Please read Daniel's essay under Identity, page 14, for his adoption story.)

I chose to write about the stuck spot LOYALTY because I know now that it has always influenced my friendships, my choices, and my decision about whether or not to open up to someone. I have also come to realize that issues around loyalty were one of the main reasons for the anger and frustration I have experienced in my life, which sometimes resulted in challenges in my relationship with my parents.

As it pertains to adoption, loyalty has been complicated for me to think about. Many adoptees feel conflicted about whether they owe loyalty to their adoptive family or their birth family. Some adoptees may believe they are being disloyal to their adoptive parents if they think about their birth families or experience other confusing emotions. Each adoption and each adoptee is different.

I did not feel this way. I never felt that I had to choose one family or the other. I never questioned my loyalty to my adoptive family. I have always clearly felt a debt of gratitude for the unconditional love and opportunities they have given me. However, when I think about my birth family, it gets confusing. There is a natural instinct to feel loyalty to my birth family that I can't begin to understand. I ask myself, *Why do I still feel as though I owe something to people who didn't protect me and put me in an abusive situation? Why do I feel that I owe loyalty to the family that gave me life instead of **only** the one that gave me a life worth living?*

It baffles me, but out of instinct, I suppose, I have spent the past 17 years with my adoptive family teaching myself to ignore and suppress my complicated feelings toward my past and my birth parents. The unfortunate consequence of this choice to bury these feelings has been that I have taken them out on my adoptive parents. My intense feelings of loss, grief, and anger ended up being directed at them and it caused many years of turmoil in my family.

I have been in both individual and family therapy since I was young. Fortunately, my parents ignored every one of my arguments against any type of therapy. I have managed to conclude that therapy has been a source of relief for my pent-up feelings of frustration and has helped to keep my family together. Therapy can help people understand how teenage issues are related, at least in part, to conflicting loyalty or other adoption-related issues that make adoptees feel mad and sad all the time, which they vent to their families. As a third party, our therapist could mediate the situation while also keeping us on topic. I never felt as if I HAD to say anything, or COULDN'T say anything. Counseling provided a place where I could be honest with my family and myself. While it wasn't easy at times, it was helpful to feel as though I had an adult in my corner who just wanted us to communicate, no matter what was said.

If I knew then what I do now, I would do things differently. My advice to other adopted kids in similar situations, is to not keep your feelings about loyalty hidden away. It might not be easy to talk about and may be frustrating or awkward at times, but it beats the alternative of keeping it inside. Parents and therapists can help you understand and untangle your feelings. When you have strong emotions, and try to keep them in, they eventually do come out. In my case, they came out in the form of anger that, at times, hurt my relationship with my adoptive parents.

On the other hand, I am thankful that my parents and therapist never forced me to express my feelings until I was ready. I have learned to accept and cope with my feelings in my own way. I am glad that I can write about my experiences with the hope that it will help other adopted teens and their parents. Sometimes people just need time to sit and understand what has happened to them without anyone trying to speed the process along. Other times, people may need a push to get out of their shell and talk about what needs to be talked about. It may be obvious, but no one is the same, no one has the same experiences as another person, and different people have different coping strategies. My biggest fear is that a parent reading this either will assume they shouldn't talk to their child or should push them to talk. It's a delicate balance of feeling out the situation to understand what their child needs. Either way, every kid needs to feel as though their parent is in their corner.

I am currently a junior in college, majoring in hospitality and minoring in communications.

Daniel

Zoe, 24

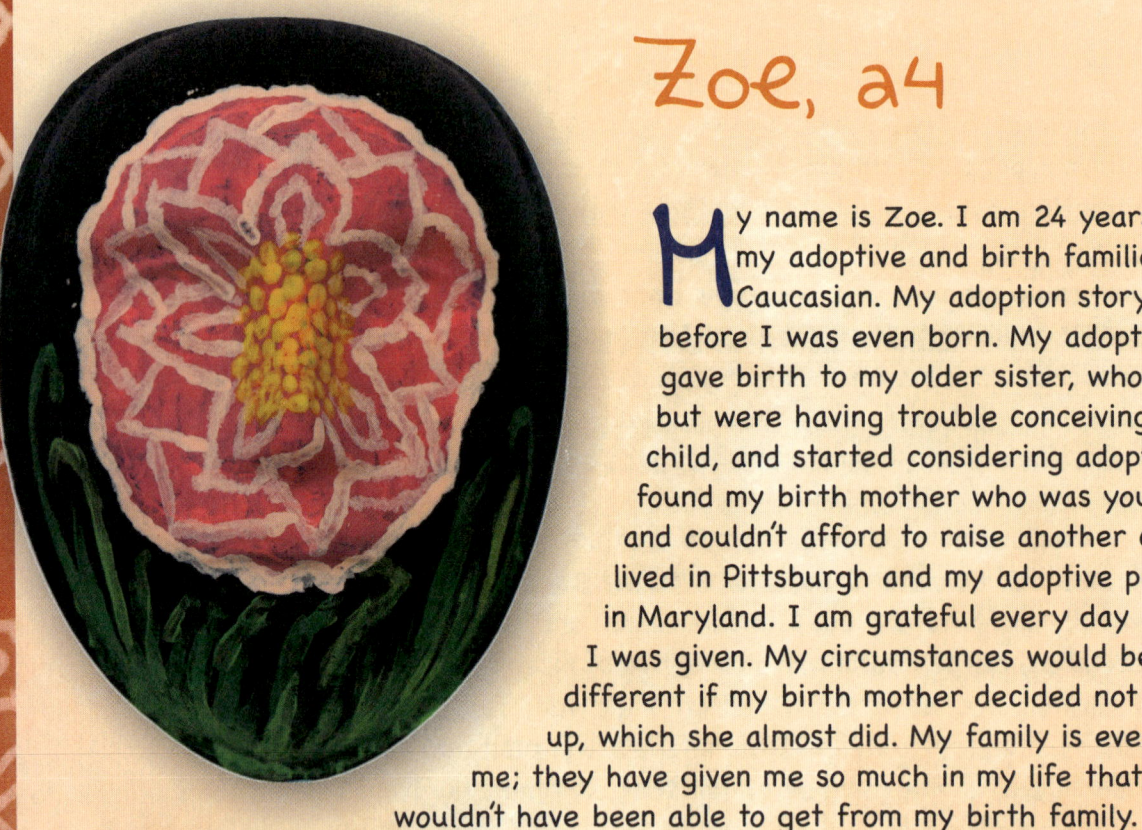

My name is Zoe. I am 24 years old and my adoptive and birth families are both Caucasian. My adoption story started before I was even born. My adoptive parents gave birth to my older sister, who is now 29, but were having trouble conceiving a second child, and started considering adoption. They found my birth mother who was young, pregnant, and couldn't afford to raise another child. She lived in Pittsburgh and my adoptive parents were in Maryland. I am grateful every day for the family I was given. My circumstances would be extremely different if my birth mother decided not to give me up, which she almost did. My family is everything to me; they have given me so much in my life that I probably wouldn't have been able to get from my birth family.

A few years after I was adopted, my birth mother became pregnant again, and again decided that she could not keep the baby. My parents adopted my sister, too. After that, my parents gave birth to my youngest sister, who is now 20.

My parents never kept our adoption a secret and while we were growing up they wanted us to know as much as we wanted to know about our adoption. My sister and I attended C.A.S.E.'s annual KAN (Kids' Adoption Network) conference. My mom always let us know that my birth mom asked about us often. For a while I was pen pals with my birth sister, who was being raised by my birth mom in Pittsburgh. To me, being adopted was the coolest thing and I shared it with everyone. It was one of the first things I would say when I met new people and I still use it as a fun fact when sharing in new groups of people.

Most adopted people would love to have the opportunity to grow up with a birth sibling and have them to relate to when times were tough. But that was not always the case with my sister because of our differences. While I was always extremely grateful for my family and never really had the desire to know my birth family, my sister did not feel the same way. Being adopted left my sister feeling unwanted, while I always felt loved. She was always looking for greener grass, thinking things would have been better in our birth family, while I knew my life was better with my adoptive family. The truth is that many adoptees may feel the way my sister did, but she has mental health challenges that exacerbated these feelings and resulted in serious behavioral challenges, which took its toll on my entire family.

The adoption agreement stated that my sister and I could meet our birth family when we turned 18. When I turned 18, I decided not to meet them. I didn't need the complication in my life; I knew who my family was. However, my parents decided to have my sister meet our birth family before she was 18 in the hope that this would help her with her problems. They hoped that knowing them and what they were like would help my sister with her sense of belonging. Unfortunately, it did not. And for me, learning that other members of my birth family might also have mental health issues was very hard for me to deal with. I went through several very difficult years. I questioned my own mental health because of my birth family's history, questioned if I even wanted to have children of my own one day given the possibility of them having mental health issues.

In addition to these worries, I struggled with so many mixed feelings toward my sister. We didn't get along great when I was younger and those problems only worsened as we grew older. But in the end, she was my birth sister. No matter how angry and upset I became with her, I was constantly told by my parents that she is my sister and I should love and support her. When her problems started to adversely affect my family, I felt enormous pressure to have a connection with her and to try to help her. When it got to be too much, I threw myself into my studies or my theatre work and tried to ignore everything that was going on at home. I thought that if I could just keep busy and be the best that I could be, I could separate myself completely from that connection with her and the responsibility to make her better. I was constantly struggling with the pressure to "be there" for my sister while also wanting to just leave it all behind me and not deal with it at all.

My mom was there for me during this very challenging time when all the questions and worries about my own mental health started coming up for me. She understood that while my sister was having a difficult time, seeing her problems and learning my birth family history was just as difficult for me. My mom supported me and always talked with me about anything that was on my mind. It took a while for me to understand that I am, in fact, not like my birth family and that is okay. I do not have the same mental health issues my sister has. I am happy with where I am in my life and the successes I have had. I found something I love to do in theatre and am actively pursuing it. I love my family with all my heart and know the grass is greener here.

I would like other adoptees to know that it is perfectly normal to feel like you want/need to meet your birth family one day. It is ALSO perfectly normal to feel like you don't have to meet them. And most importantly, it is YOUR decision whether or not to meet them. Today, it is easier to locate birth family members because of social media, the Internet, and the different ancestry tests and websites available. But none of these opportunities should make you feel compelled to have contact with your birth family if you don't want to. To this day, I still get messages from my birth family wanting to connect, but I know what I want and I know who I am without them. Sometimes you just need to find your patch of green grass to know you're okay, whether that patch of green grass is right there with your adoptive family, with your birth family, or somewhere in between, with both families integrated into your life. And only you can make that decision for yourself.

Zoe

Activity

Personal Constellation

Sometimes it may seem as if you must choose between the different people in your life, or choose between birth and adoptive families. What happens if instead you think about the people who are in your life and those who may come and go in your life as part of your personal constellation? Fill in the stars and planets below to create the constellation of your universe. You are in the center, the sun, in this constellation. Who is orbiting around you? Think about your family—your adoptive family and your birth family. Where would you put them? Think about who you turn to and depend on for different things and assign them to one of the surrounding stars or planets. Who do you talk to when you've had a hard day? Who would you call if you were in trouble? If you have two movie tickets, who do you take with you? When you want to talk about adoption, who do you talk to? If you want or need to, add more planets.

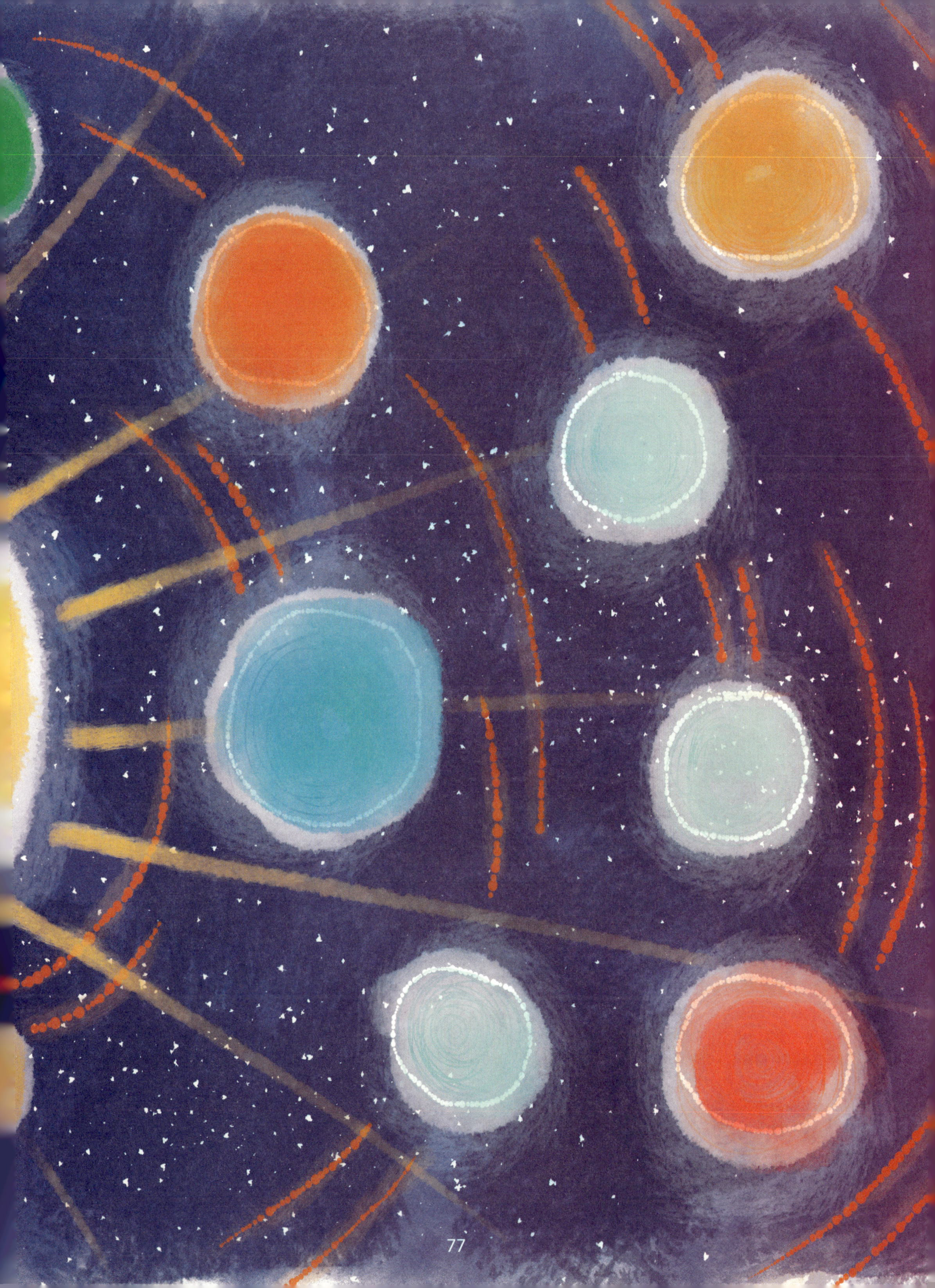

Journal Reflections on Connections

Look at your constellation. What are your thoughts? Do you feel like there are too many or too few people in your universe? Which connections would you like to be stronger? Who are the most important people in your universe? Do you ever feel conflicted about your loyalty to your birth and adoptive families?

_____
_____
_____
_____
_____
_____
_____
_____
_____
_____
_____
_____
_____
_____
_____
_____
_____
_____
_____
_____
_____
_____
_____
_____
_____
_____

Journal Reflections on Connections

Journal...continued

Exercise Balloon

Close your eyes and imagine that you have a balloon of your favorite color.

As you blow it up, you are going to imagine that every upsetting, unhappy, and unwanted thought or feeling is leaving you and going into the balloon. With each breath, the balloon gets bigger and your thoughts and feelings become calmer.

When you have all your upset outside of you and in the balloon, you can tie it off and let it go. It gently rises into the sky and out of sight, taking your distress with it. Once out of sight, it dissolves into the nothingness of space, leaving no residue to pollute the earth or to continue to upset you in any way.

Permanence

"If my birth parents gave me away, it could happen again."

"I've lived in so many foster homes, I'm sure I'll be moved again."

"I'll be 18 soon. Will my parents still be there for me after I leave home?"

Whether you were placed for adoption as an infant or lived in an orphanage or foster homes before joining your adoptive family, adoption means that you are not living with the people who gave birth to you. Someone made an adoption plan or you were removed because it was not safe for you to remain with your birth family. For many teens, this realization can create a feeling of uncertainty or insecurity in their adoptive family. If one set of parents "gave me away, didn't want me, or try to keep me, how do I know it will not happen again?" Maybe you worry that if your behavior is unacceptable, and your parents are angry with you, they will have you leave. If you have experienced multiple moves in foster care, or pre-adoption placements that did not work out, struggles with this spot may feel justified to you. Maybe you have wondered if your parents will still be your parents once the "parenting role" is over and you enter young adulthood.

Teresa, Naomi, and Annabeth share their fears of losing their adoptive parents and their struggle to feel a secure sense of belonging in their families.

Teresa, 16

My name is Teresa and I am 16 years old. I was born in Manila, Philippines and I lived there for the first two years of my life. During those two years, I moved several times between the orphanage and foster care homes. I was finally lucky to be placed with Mama Rose and her family. I thought they were going to be my forever family, but I was wrong. That is why I chose to write about "permanency." I lived with Mama Rose and her family for two years, and they were all that I knew.

One day, these strange people came. My adoptive mom looked like everyone else I knew, but my adoptive dad looked a little different, his skin was much paler than anyone's I had ever seen before. After meeting my parents, the next thing I knew we were driving away in a van and Mama Rose was sprinting after us like her feet were on fire. We stopped and Mama Rose was holding my Red Pillow, the only thing that I truly owned at the time. I always slept with Red Pillow and it was my safety when things got tough for me. Mama Rose told my parents that I needed to have Red Pillow on my journey. Of course, I don't completely remember this interaction.

What I do remember is later that night, my mom and her friend went to the mall to buy me clothes and I stayed at the hotel with my dad. We were having fun running around the hotel room, but then suddenly, I wanted to go home. My dad couldn't understand what I was saying, but he understood what was happening. I kicked, I screamed, I spit, and I tried to escape. I wanted to go back to Mama Rose, my family. For the next several years that's what I did whenever I was upset. I kicked, I screamed, I spit, and tried to escape. The only thing that ever seemed to calm me was Red Pillow.

As I grew a little older the topic of adoption always seemed to shut me down. I would try to pretend that I wasn't adopted, that I hadn't left anyone behind, and that my adoptive parents were my "real" parents. Needless to say, this pretending often affected my mood. Mom and Dad were worried about me so they started consulting with many professionals, including a psychiatrist.

The psychiatrist advised my parents to have me hospitalized and have my head shaved to prevent me from pulling my hair out. This doctor told my dad that I simply needed to learn to behave.

My father decided this advice felt very wrong, so he began an Internet search to find help specifically for adoptive families. He called C.A.S.E. and talked to a therapist for more than an hour. She has been my family's therapist since that day. For the record, I have never been hospitalized and my hair has never looked better.

My therapist helped me learn how to grieve for all my past losses and helped me realize that you can't always control how your story begins, but you have the power to influence how it ends. She understood how traumatic it was for me to leave the only home I had ever known. My family and I learned how to communicate without hurting each other's feelings. I learned to not be afraid to use my own voice, not only at home but out in the world, which helped transform me into the strong leader that I am today.

Two years ago, I faced one of my biggest fears, putting myself out there for everyone to see, and I sang for the first time in public. This experience increased my self-confidence. That scared little girl from the Philippines could never have done that without my amazing therapist, and my special family who truly is my forever home. I still have Red Pillow, though a bit tattered, to remember the things and people I've lost.

Teresa B.

Naomi, 23

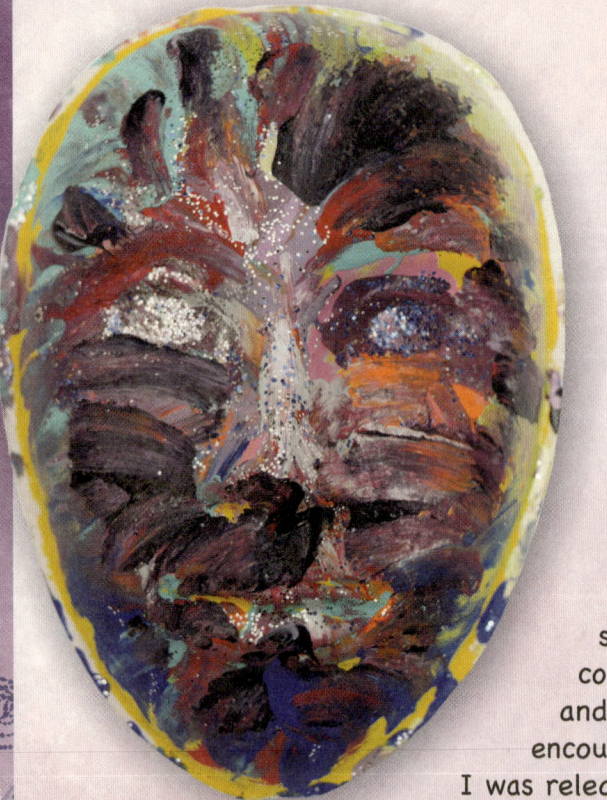

Hello, my name is Naomi and I am a 23-year-old African-American woman who was adopted by my single, Caucasian mother when I was only three weeks old. I don't remember my birth parents at all. My mom has always been very open with both my brother and me about our adoptions. She did her best to answer any questions that we had. From what my mom has told me about my adoption, I was placed for adoption after I was born because my birth mom realized that she could not take care of me. There were several reasons for her decision. My birth mom already had several other children, and she suffered from a serious drug problem that she couldn't kick. I was born addicted to drugs. The doctor and hospital staff were concerned for my well-being and encouraged my birth mother to make an adoption plan. After I was released from the hospital, I couldn't go home with my adoptive mom because my birth father had refused to sign the papers that would relinquish his parental rights. And then he just disappeared and could not be found. I was placed in a foster home for three weeks. Finally, everything was resolved and I could go home to my mother.

The stuck spot that I have struggled with the most has been permanence, primarily during 3rd through 10th grades. Especially when I was younger, I would have terrifying thoughts that if I wasn't good enough, my mom wouldn't want me anymore and would want to give me up. These thoughts would come into my head whenever I found myself struggling academically in school, and whenever my mom and I would have a fight. These terrible thoughts were compounded on a few occasions when another kid would ask me if I was scared that my mom would want to give me back to my "real" family. And honestly, when I was in elementary school, it was a thought that terrified me almost all the time.

I had a very hard time in school; I have ADHD and dyslexia. It was difficult for me to focus and learn, especially math. There were basic skills that I should have been able to master, but I couldn't. This left me feeling terrified that my mom would think that I was a useless waste of time and that she would want to give me back. However, I think I was especially terrified that my mom would try to give me back to my birth mother and that my birth mother would not want me either, and then I would end up alone with no family.

As I grew older, I was able to share my fears with my mother, and while talking made me feel a bit better, it didn't entirely silence my fears. I realized that my thoughts and feelings had shifted from fear to depression. I know this was an irrational response because I knew in my heart that my mother loved me, but my brain hadn't quite figured that out yet. When I entered middle school and later high school, I learned how to talk myself down whenever I was having a really hard time with my thoughts. In middle school, my academic struggles triggered my depression. So pretty much, I was struggling the entire time that I was in school. Finally, the positive change came at the end of my 10th grade year/beginning of 11th grade; somehow, I realized that I was safe in my house and that there was no way that my mom would even think about giving me up. She would always tell me when I was having a depressive episode, "Honey, I want you to know and always remember that I will love you, no matter what. No matter what you are going through and no matter what happens between us, there is nothing that you can do to get rid of me."

To combat my fears and depression, as I was growing up I needed different types of help. In elementary school it really helped going to C.A.S.E. and talking with the wonderful women who worked there. They created a safe space and reassured me that my feelings were normal and that I had nothing to worry about. They helped me figure out the best way to share my feelings with my mom and other people in my life, like my teachers, if I needed to.

It was more difficult in middle and high school to talk about my feelings because I believed they did not seem legitimate. I felt that I shouldn't burden others with my problems and I should be able to figure out how to handle them all by myself. When I was in 10th grade, my mom found a therapist for me and I saw her for three years. At first, it did make things better, being able to talk to someone who hadn't known me for my entire life, someone who could have a non-biased opinion. However, after a time, I realized that I began to feel uncomfortable talking to her about the more personal things that were going on with me. And this realization was very painful because it reflected one of my worst fears: someone coming into my life who I form a connection with, with whom I share my deepest fears and feelings, and then one day I no longer feel that connection, and then they just go away. At this point in my life, I no longer worry about my mom not wanting me. However, I now worry sometimes that significant others or friends who I really care about will leave me. This feels even worse because friends and lovers are not obligated to love you. Sometimes I feel like I keep having to fight to make friends, trying to prove that I am worthy of their time. I know I need to keep working on this…I am still a work in progress.

My involvement in sports helped me most of all. I may not have done well academically, but I really excelled at sports, especially Track and Field. Team sports provided me with one of the few places where I could fit in. People noticed me and cared. It was one place where I felt like I couldn't fail, and even when I did, everyone was still proud of me instead of being disappointed.

My advice for the teens: If you ever find yourself having doubts about your parents' love for you, either find someone whom you can trust to talk to, or find a comfortable way to express yourself, through writing, drawing, dancing, or songwriting. Knowing you can share your feelings may help you feel better. You may also want to find an enjoyable activity to take your mind off your troubles, even if it is just for a little while. Oh, by the way, drugs don't count as an activity.

In summary, I hope you can find a place where you feel safe and where you feel like you can be yourself. Don't think that just because you feel upset or worried now, that things will stay that way forever and you will never be able to move past it. It will get better.

Thanks for reading.

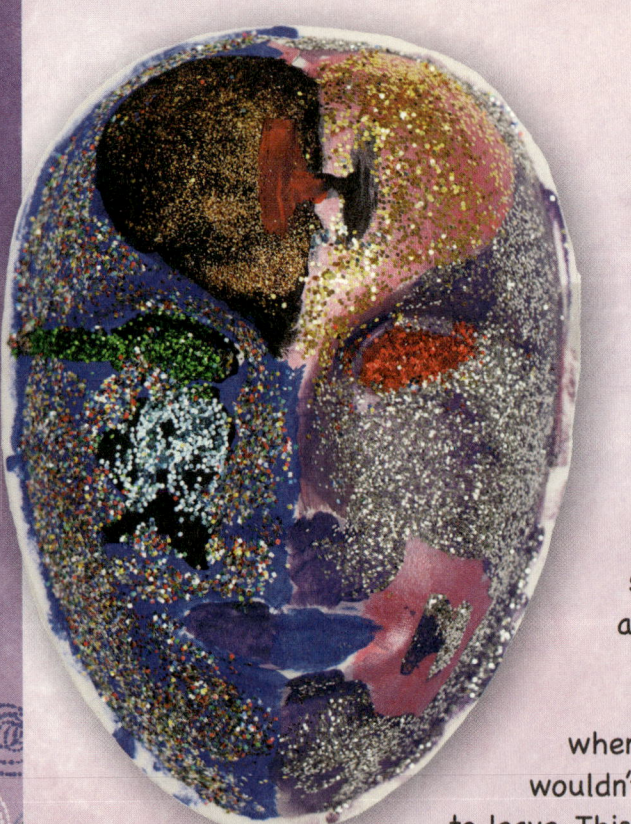

Annabeth, 13

My name is Annabeth and I am 13 years old. I lived with my birth family in Maine and New York until I was seven years old. I was taken away because I wasn't safe. I went to live in a foster home for five years. Then I met Liesel and Casey, who adopted my younger sister and me in December 2017. My birth and adoptive families are Caucasian.

I am writing about permanence because when I joined my adoptive family, I was afraid it wouldn't work out and my sister and I would have to leave. This is because it was hard for me to trust Liesel and Casey. I didn't trust them because the last few people who I did trust were not trustworthy; they left me. Before Casey and Liesel, when I was living in my foster home in New York, there was a couple who was supposed to adopt me and my little sister. We visited them twice, and they decided not to adopt us. I felt sad and rejected. I lost my birth family, then I lost the people who were supposed to adopt me, then I moved away from my foster mom. I was afraid Liesel and Casey would change their minds and send me back to foster care. I felt very bad about myself, like I was trash.

I started to misbehave in my new home. Not right away, but a few months after living there. I did the opposite of what my parents asked me to do or I just refused to do things they asked me to do. I yelled at them. I had meltdowns over little things. I acted like I didn't care about them even though I did. When I started school in my new home, I was on the honor roll, but then I started to fall behind. My grades started to drop. My parents tried to help me, but I pushed them away and told them to leave me alone.

We began seeing a therapist who has helped me begin to learn how to control my emotions and learn to trust. My parents have helped me by talking to me, hugging me and not giving up on me. It was very difficult, but I finally talked to them about how hard it has been to trust them.

I still sometimes worry that I will be taken away, but not nearly as often. I know in my head it won't happen, but I feel that way sometimes. I am working on building trust by asking for help when I need it. It is still hard to control my anger sometimes, but I am really trying to do a better job because I have people to help me.

I am a seventh grader and I am good in math. I play football and lacrosse, and I like reading. I also love to do art.

The message I want other kids in similar situations to know is that it may be very scary, but let the grownups help you by telling them what frightens and worries you. Your adoptive parents may feel like strangers at first, but pay attention and find out who they are, and you will likely see how nice they are.

Annabeth

Activity: Graffiti on Boulder

What is permanent in your life? Use a marker to write it on the boulder, graffiti-style if you like. Consider people, feelings, talents, attributes.

ART   REAL   FUN

PLAY   STYLE

"ROCK"

NO

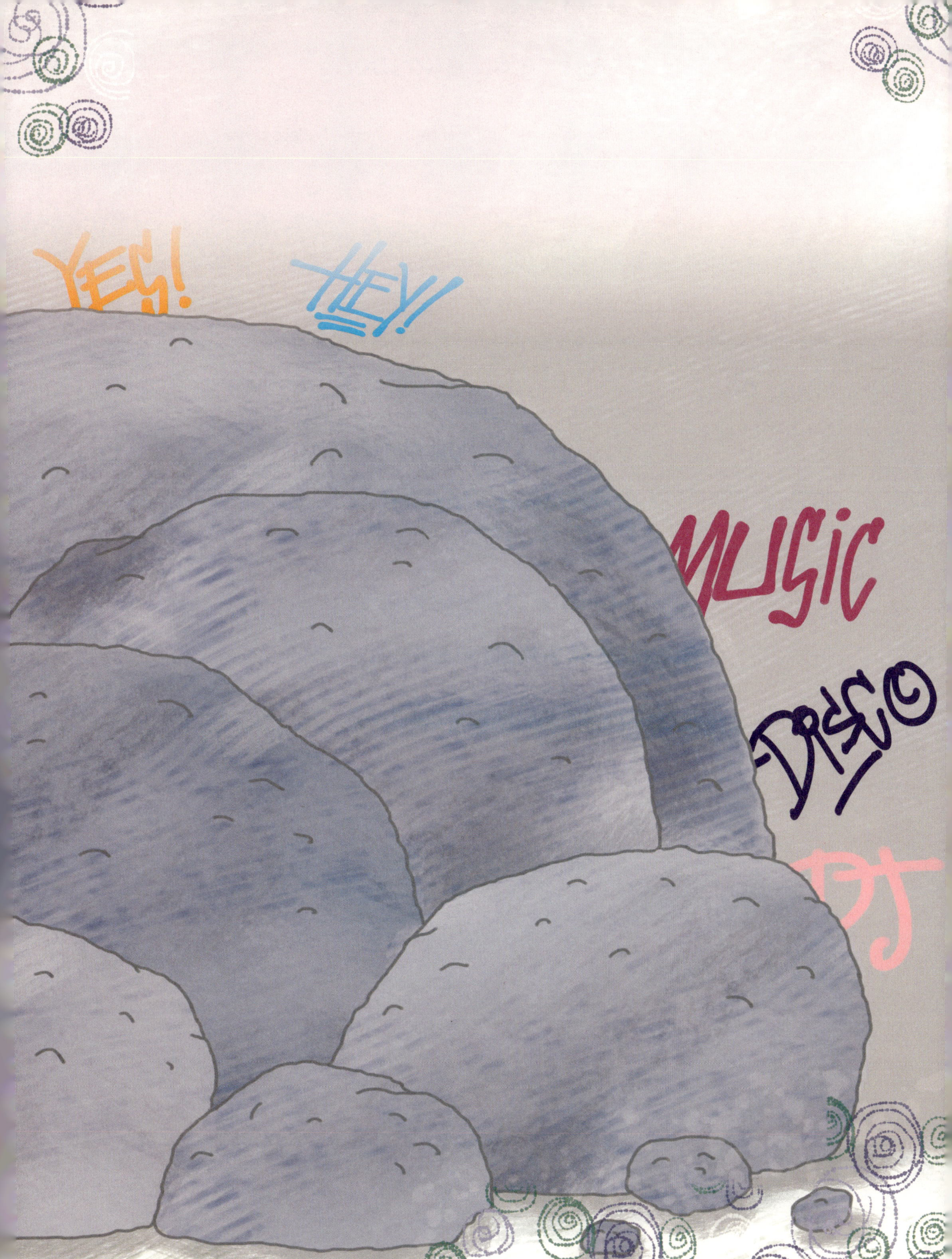
YES!
HEY!
MUSIC
DISCO
DJ

Journal What Feels Permanent

How has being adopted affected your sense of permanence? Were there permanent things in your life that you lost?

Journal...continued

Journal...continued

Exercise: Letter From Your Future Self

Can you remember a time when you were younger and worried about something that seemed so difficult at the time that now seems almost silly? As you grow, you gain important insight, experience, and maturity that help you cope with life. Write a letter from future you—5 or 10 years older than you are now—to the current you. What would the letter say? What advice would you give? What reassurance?

Dear _____
your name

Final Thoughts

We hope you found the real-life stories and the interactive exercises in this book helpful.

Spread the word

Please share with other adoptees you know who could benefit from this book as well. This book can be purchased on Amazon or C.A.S.E.'s website at www.adoptionsupport.org.

Tell us what you think

- Write a review of this book at www.adoptionsupport.org/store/teens
- Email us at teens@adoptionsupport.org

We remain forever grateful to the wonderful young adoptees who shared their personal stories to make this book possible.

All the best,
The C.A.S.E. Team

Notes, scribbles, doodles, etc.

About C.A.S.E.

The Center for Adoption Support and Education (C.A.S.E.) is a national leader in mental health services for the foster care and adoption community both locally and nationwide. C.A.S.E. improves the lives of children who have been adopted or in foster care and their families through counseling, lifelong education, and a growing national network of trained professionals. With five offices across the Washington, D.C. Metro Area and a wealth of educational resources, webinars and training opportunities, C.A.S.E. nurtures, inspires, and empowers all those touched by adoption.

Beneath the Mask: For Teen Adoptees was made possible in part by funding from The Pederson Family and individuals like you. If you found this workbook useful, please help C.A.S.E. provide support to adoptive families searching for answers. Visit C.A.S.E. online at www.adoptionsupport.org to make a donation, find an adoption-competent therapist, download free resources, register for engaging webinars, and purchase popular publications like the *W.I.S.E. Up! Powerbook*, *Beneath the Mask: Understanding Adopted Teens*, and *The Whole Me*.

C.A.S.E.
the nonprofit
CENTER FOR ADOPTION
SUPPORT AND EDUCATION
since 1998

nurture.
inspire.
empower.